A SEASON of DEATH

A SEASON of DEATH

A memoir

MARK RAPHAEL BAKER

For Melila

To every thing there is a season,
and a time to every purpose under the heaven:
A time to be born, a time to die;
a time to plant, and a time to pluck up that which is planted;
A time to kill, and a time to heal;
a time to break down, and a time to build up;
A time to weep, and a time to laugh;
a time to mourn, and a time to dance;
A time to cast away stones, and a time to gather stones together;
a time to embrace, and a time to refrain from embracing;
A time to get, and a time to lose;
a time to keep, and a time to cast away;
A time to rend, and a time to sew;
a time to keep silence, and a time to speak;
A time to love, and a time to hate;
A time of war, and a time of peace.

Ecclesiastes 3:1–8

Rabbi Levi said: At the time the soul leaves the body, a voice goes from one end of the world to the other end–and even though people are sitting nearby, they do not hear.

Exodus Rabbah 5:9

Melbourne University Publishing acknowledges the traditional owners of the unceded land on which we work, learn and live: the Wurundjeri Woi-wurrung peoples of the Kulin nation. We pay respect to elders past, present and future, and acknowledge the importance of Indigenous knowledge.

MELBOURNE UNIVERSITY PRESS
An imprint of Melbourne University Publishing Limited
Level 1, 715 Swanston Street, Carlton, Victoria 3053, Australia
mup-contact@unimelb.edu.au
www.mup.com.au

First published 2024

Cover design by Pfisterer + Freeman
Typeset by Adala Studio
Cover artwork 'glasses' 2023 courtesy Anita Lester
Printed in China by 1010 Printing International Limited

9780522880892 (paperback)
9780522880908 (ebook)

CONTENTS

REGENERATION

I

THE SAGES teach, 'From where do we come?' to which they spit out the answer, 'From a place of putrid water.'

'And where are we headed?' they deign to ask, followed by a response that proves they are none other than the Angel of Death in scholarly camouflage: 'To a place of worms and maggots.'

But lest we forget, they add the punchline: all that stands before each of us at the end of our days is a mirror in which we see our reflection from birth to death.

This is what I see in the mirror as my luvluv, the Hebrew word for pancreas, spreads its poison through my disfigured body. I can barely recognise myself. An impossible play of words, a reversal of meanings. LoveLove.

Look, before I am devoured by the earth of my grave where my beginnings and ends meet. Remember the imperative, repeated in the Bible 269 times: 'Zachor! Gedenk! Remember!' Or as offered by an esoteric teaching of the Greek mystery schools: 'Die before you die so that when you die you won't die.'

My words will protect me, laid in earth.

Remember me! Remember me!

2

MY SEASON of death began with my wife of thirty-three years, mother to our three children. Kerryn was ready to face middle age in her fifties when an innocuous stomach-ache turned out to be the rarest of gastric cancers. The gastroenterologist warned us to avoid a consultation with Dr Google, but it didn't stop me from staring that night at the forecasts. They all converged on the same verdict: a year would be lucky. Only a stomach resection could alter the decree. I didn't even know what a resection meant and followed the web through the links until I came to some anatomical illustrations.

Kerryn's next appointment was with a surgeon. In the eyes of our family, who crowded into the room, he was a god—a god who, through no fault of his own, used his instruments to penetrate the innards of Kerryn's abdomen, only to emerge in blue robes with a solemn face. 'I'm afraid there's nothing I can do.'

His estimation in the eyes of my children fell from god to broken idol, though we continued to hold onto a glimmer of hope that the idol could be restored and perform his magic. The surgeon promised he'd do his best. It was the last time we saw him.

Within a week, the cancer had moved from an invisible presence to a subterranean force that fought for the lead role in the orchestral percussions of Kerryn's churning stomach. It trumpeted its arrival by inflicting excruciating pain, immobilising one leg, so that by the time we reached the stage of her first chemotherapy, she could barely manage the pain laid upon a hospital bed.

There followed a period of ten months during which Kerryn chose her own way of confronting her impending death. Everyone spoke of her grace, the way she opened our house to friends, never once expressed anger and spoke openly about her parents. Three decades had elapsed since her parents' deaths and now it was Kerryn's turn to face her own early dying. She knew that family and friends were desperate to show their love for her, but understood as a therapist that it was we who needed to be showered with her love, which could never be sated. She spoke to each of the children about their future, organised an engagement party for our son Gabe and his fiancée, Gabi, and delivered a speech that was described as heroic, filled with humour, though she was a dying woman.

After her death, I went home from the hospice with my children and for seven days we practised the Jewish rites of Shiva, but in our own way, inviting a yoga teacher to conduct a session on a mat, which ended with 'om' and the recitation of the Kaddish. I was haunted by bearing witness to Kerryn's death; we had watched her breaths quicken and slow, we had screamed in horror when her chest lifted and, like a ghost from the *Exorcist*, she took one breath, followed by a final gasp, before flopping onto the pillow, breathless forever.

That experience followed me; every breath I took felt like Kerryn's last breath. The source of life, inhaling and exhaling, mimicked her demise. Death and life became inextricably bound; I was unsure which world I belonged to, and in my dreams at night I danced with her spirit, sang the songs of our courtship, reanimated her in my mind and eventually rushed to write a version of our life story, which I completed in thirty days.

For the remainder of the year, I reshaped those words as though its letters were creating a golem, that mythical creature of clay first moulded in sixteenth-century Prague. I escaped our home and travelled to isolated islands where I swam in phosphorescent waters inverting day and night, light and darkness, as though in imitation of the tilt of my heart, tethered between that stifled last gasp and the ones I trusted to revivify me.

It was in those waters that I learned to breathe again, during a yoga retreat where we began each morning practising breathing and stillness looking over the Aegean Sea. For the first time, through the company of strangers, I listened to the stories of others and became more open to life.

After ten months of mourning following Kerryn's death, in addition to the ten months of grief that had consumed me during Kerryn's illness, I was ready to reconnect with a world that felt foreign—the world of the living. I became engaged again with the lives of other people and joined an ad hoc club of widows and widowers, a small circle that had turned their own losses into artistic endeavours. I felt with my book I was part of them, and even went on one or two dates, where I floundered like a child and mangled my lines, for it had been thirty-two years since I had last asked someone out. Still, I persisted, determined to leave behind the land of the dead.

3

TEN MONTHS had passed since Kerryn's death. I was out for a weekly dinner with my brother, Johnny—five years older than me—and two intimate friends, where over drinks we convened our private parliament as if we could change the course of world politics, especially those of Israel–Palestine. My worldview was further to the left than my brother's, who scoffed that we argued on the head of a pin about the one per cent we disagreed on, while I insisted it was ninety-nine per cent.

This time we avoided politics because the conversation quickly focused on my brother's complaints about a persistent pain in his back for which he'd had an MRI that day. We were surprisingly joined halfway through the meal by a medical friend who was supposed to be celebrating his wedding anniversary. I recall judging him, or rather his marriage, for abandoning his wife to dine with his mates. At the end of the meal, he insisted on driving my brother home.

No one raised an eyebrow. The following morning I received a call from Johnny. My judgements about his medical friend had been totally misdirected. His companion had joined us for dinner to tell my brother news that had nothing to do with his own marriage. The radiologist had found a suspicious shadow while doing the MRI on Johnny's back. His medical friend had already arranged an appointment for a PET scan. Johnny could have chosen anyone to accompany him, but he wanted me. I'm not sure that he intuited an outcome whose trail I could help him navigate, or if it was just that he trusted me. He was certainly fearful. I was shocked; was it possible that cancer was stealing an encore?

I would never have known what a PET scan was, among all the other zoological X-rays such as the CAT scan, if it was not for Kerryn's cancer. This one highlights tumour activity using a colourful radioactive image. It was targeted on Johnny's lower oesophagus, which medical anatomy categorised as an upper gastrointestinal zone. The radiologist knew Johnny personally, which led him to divulge results that normally require a delay of days. The flashing traffic lights confirmed a tumour on his gullet, or lower oesophagus.

Within a day or so we were back in the offices of the same oncologist who had treated Kerryn, prompting me to quote from *The Shining* at its climactic moment of horror, 'Heeere's Johnny!'

The language was painfully familiar. I knew immediately what he was about to say, though I wished I didn't. 'I'm not going to give you a prognosis because statistically there are always outliers, but you're going to die from this.'

It surely was not possible that our family was being hit once again by a terminal cancer in such a short period of time. In a world where multitudes suffer from war and mass murder, I nonetheless felt it to be cruel to Johnny and his family, and doubly cruel to my parents, who had endured the worst travails of the Holocaust in their youths, yet rebuilt a stable and loving family in Australia.

Satan! I wanted to shout at that mythical creature of evil, take your arse to someone else—as if the misfortune of a family can be magically rectified by a hollow Jobian lament.

4

IT'S IMPOSSIBLE to untangle my regeneration and early courtship of Michelle from the news about my brother. She was no stranger to me. Twenty years younger, she had a long association with Johnny's children. During her final years at school, her boyfriend was my nephew Nadav, whom I had held in my arms when he was a child.

After she and Nadav broke up, they went their different ways. He married and had kids; she moved on to other relationships. They had little contact, but Michelle stayed attached to the family, mainly through Nadav's elder sister Timnah, who became her close friend. She was embedded in the Baker family, playing a formative role as a 'sister' to my youngest niece, Karni, and a confidante to others. She was particularly close to Johnny, who sought out her company and opinion on Israeli affairs during his annual visits to Israel, where she lived and showed him the coolest cafes in Tel Aviv. In her eyes, I was Uncle Marky.

I also came to know Michelle independently at university, where she topped classes in the department that I would eventually head. While doing her PhD, she lectured in subjects I taught, with a strong interest in the Arab–Israeli conflict and the Holocaust, both areas central to my research interests. As director of the Australian Centre for Jewish Civilisation at Monash University, I regularly took students on overseas study trips to zones of trauma—Rwanda and sites of Holocaust memory in Europe. One of the trips to Israel and Palestine was called 'War and Peace'. I needed help and Michelle happened to be on holiday leave from writing an independent report on military accountability and the laws of war. As one of the academic instructors, she gave lectures to the students on international law and politics, and used her network of contacts to organise political commentators and a visit to the Israeli Supreme Court where the group heard from one of the judges.

Kerryn came on this and other trips as a therapist for the students. The three of us—Michelle, Kerryn and I—often sat at the same dinner table or went out to a restaurant together, where we bonded over gossip and our common ties in Australia. During a visit home at the peak of Kerryn's illness, Michelle visited Kerryn. Kerryn wasn't well enough to eat but the three of us sat at the kitchen table while Michelle and I ate spaghetti bolognese, reminiscing about our trip to Israel, as if nothing had changed.

But everything had changed. Michelle recalls leaving our house thinking not only about the inevitability of Kerryn's death, but also about the way my own life would forever be marred by grief.

Kerryn had told me repeatedly when she was dying that she wanted me to marry in the future, adding one condition: 'Don't marry a bitch.' Although at the time I couldn't imagine a new relationship, Kerryn's act of generosity and selflessness helped me open up to the prospect of one day breaking out of my state of mourning.

When Timnah told me that Michelle was thinking about returning from Israel to Australia for an extended visit, I started writing WhatsApp messages to her under the pretence of a liaison based only on our mutual interests in politics—specifically, about Obama's condemnation of Israeli settlements in a UN resolution that we both supported. It seemed innocent enough to Michelle; nothing to raise her suspicions.

Then came the messages about Johnny's diagnosis. In one note I have archived, I prodded her about whether she was planning a return trip: 'So are you still coming to Australia to save us?'

'Undecided,' she answered. 'I'm still trying to work out what will save me.'

Our contact continued when she took charge of Karni, who was on a program in Israel and broke to her the news about Johnny's cancer.

Afraid to admit my romantic aspirations, I hid my pursuit of her through various covert ways that focused on how our interests converged. We both received simultaneous alert beeps on our phones from the same news sources. During the years away she developed a CV that so impressed me that I regarded it in the manner a traditional matchmaker would scrutinise the merits of a prospective bride or groom. I didn't stop to think about the chutzpah of presuming that she would be interested in a man twenty years her senior. Our CVs spoke for themselves and foretold a romantic liaison. Wouldn't that be enough for two pieces of a puzzle to immediately come together and snap into place? But Michelle had no interest in being loved for her CV, regardless of the crazy age differential between us. It was being in love that interested her, something that she never believed was possible with a man twenty years older than her.

I must have sounded like a nagger when I contacted Michelle the second she landed in Australia: 'Hiya and wilkommen. When's coffee or a drink one evening?'

She agreed to meet, fuelling my amorous fantasies, but I felt it was pity that drove her to meet me. It was a Saturday afternoon, when I normally wouldn't drive due to my Sabbath observance. But grief had temporarily put a hold on my religious rituals, and so she offered to pick me up in the afternoon, joking she was my Shabbas goy, a gentile who performs by proxy acts forbidden to religious Jews on the Sabbath. We went to an inner-city bar with pretences of 1920s Berlin. Its tinge of romance would set an exotic tone for our encounter. The conversation was a little strained at first, less easy than I imagined, both of us curtailing ourselves for different reasons.

I sought another way of upping the ante in the most boyish of ways, again without betraying my deeper motives. We both practised yoga and I knew she'd need a studio during her stay. I put her name down on one of those 'sign up a friend' deals and lent her some complimentary passes with the password changed to a private joke we shared: '1948vs1967', signalling the pivotal debates around Israel's occupation of Palestine. My hope was that we would choose some common class times and I would hear her pranayama breaths on an adjacent mat. Once again, she was surprised and grateful, but not enough to read my subterfuge; after all, it could have been interpreted as a gift of gratitude for caring for my family.

My bolder move came next: an invitation to dinner at an Italian restaurant. Michelle took this as a familiar combination of Baker pushiness and generosity, but her parents' suspicions were aroused when they saw me rock up in my convertible Mini Minor to their St Kilda home where she was staying. At the restaurant, called Thirty Eight Chairs, I played my own version of musical chairs, moving the conversation around our default topic of politics and then drifting into an impromptu declaration of my truer intentions. I said that Johnny had casually mentioned that he thought we'd make a good couple if I was ten years younger and she was ten years older. She laughed it off.

'I was never good at maths,' I said, trying to cover my embarrassment.

What we lacked in our verbal exchange that evening was soon replaced by a verbosity that I engineered using social media platforms. I laid down my cards, a full house of hearts, to which she countered with a closing hand of the ace of clubs.

'I don't know what you're thinking,' she silenced me, 'but we're in different worlds.' I countered by citing her work in Israel's justice system, especially in its Supreme Court, and on the report on Operation Protective Edge in Gaza.

'It's not about that stuff,' she said. 'It's about so much more. You. Me. Your grief. I feel like that's what's speaking. I think we should stop.'

But nothing could stop me. It's all recorded, my attempts to woo her, on her phone and mine, captured forever on WhatsApp messages. What gave me the confidence to believe that she would take me seriously? Was it something about my character, a narcissistic confidence that I had plied in advancing my academic career, now harnessed to the lost art of dating?

She thought my sudden turn to a romantic interest was bizarre and tried to soften the blow to my ego by reiterating that we were at different stages of our lives. She wanted children, she said again and again, reminding me that I already have my own adult kids.

I refused to give in so easily. I continued to write messages—long messages professing my sincerity.

'This is your grief talking,' she repeated. 'Can't you see we're at different stages of life?' and then, modulating her response, 'I'm happy to hang out, but …'

'I hear your BUT and accept it and respect it,' I replied, tearing through what I saw as a sign of weakness.

'I'm also grateful because you reminded me not to settle for anything in a relationship that doesn't feel one hundred per cent right. And that's important for me at this stage in my life.'

In my eyes, she was one hundred per cent right for me. I signed off, but with a message of hope that staged a surge of confidence through her ambivalence: 'Uncle Marky xx'.

5

MICHELLE WOULD later say that I wooed her with my words or, more specifically, with my self-conscious text messages. It took long weeks for her to let my affectionate screeds scrape her heart, a period during which we occasionally saw one another, sometimes with Johnny and Timnah at a restaurant.

She finally succumbed to the Big Date, or my Big Test. I felt like an adolescent again, butterflies in my tummy. How would I pass the test? What *was* the test?

First, I had to choose an impressionable venue. I decided on a trip to one of my favourite parts of Victoria, the Yarra Valley, stopping for an early lunch at a winery and then a drive through the Black Spur forest.

Second on my list of to-dos was the choice of dress. I elected to transcend my age by wearing a singlet, shorts and thongs. I realised I'd erred when I arrived and Michelle emerged in a blue frock, fitted and short. A myriad of tummy butterflies dropped into a mass grave. We pretended not to notice that in matters of dress we weren't synchronised.

We drove with my roof off so that I could make her hair blow in the wind. My belief that I had vanquished her objections via the ammunition of WhatsApp felt exhilarating. We reached our first destination at a winery, sat on the verandah and ordered pizzas and chardonnay.

It was a glorious day, the banter light. Suddenly, Michelle's face turned serious. 'There's something I need to tell you.'

What followed was a revelation that carried with it a story of her own trauma. She held her palms to her chest.

'I have the BRCA 1 mutation,' she told me.

She must have thought I was shocked.

'This is something that's really important for you to know.'

I sipped from the wine glass. 'Umm. I don't know what you're talking about.'

And I didn't. I was naive about medical terms. This wasn't how I expected our date to progress. I was failing to understand something basic that cut deep in her.

She gave me a quick lesson like a child in a grade six biology class. 'I've had a mastectomy.' She paused. 'A double.'

I stared back dumbly.

'You know, like Angelina Jolie.'

Thanks to the glamorous actress who had created public awareness that helped normalise the surgery, Michelle's reference point made it easier to explain her journey. The point of her telling me was that she was still at a high risk of ovarian cancer, given that the mutation was very strong in her family history. The risk of breast cancer, however, had been removed by the massive surgery that Michelle undertook seven years earlier when she turned thirty. The trauma was exacerbated by the break-up of a serious relationship that didn't withstand the pressure of her life-altering news.

I felt the debris of dead butterflies resurrect in my stomach (or it might have been the pizza). There was nothing in her CV that could guide me. A part of me went numb. Breast or gastric or lung cancer? I pulled myself together. I was on a date. I was ready to leave behind the mourner's club. She assured me that she had less chance of contracting breast cancer given her surgery than a person without the gene. So weren't we both in safe territory? She dropped her hands.

'I'm not worried,' I declared. I believed that I, of all people, could empathise and felt bad for everything she had endured.

Looking back, I also know she was trying to teach me a lesson, one that I was resistant to accepting. She was telling me that all my WhatsApp words were just words, that I was still a grieving mourner, that it was possible that I wasn't ready for a relationship. She said it wasn't the age difference. It was me—I needed more time. I refused to believe her. I could still vindicate myself.

We finished the wine, sheltered by the towering trees of the Black Spur forest that were more than a thousand years old. We commented on the beauty. We walked through the grass, winding our way along boulders, when I stepped out of myself and panicked. The twenty-year gap between us suddenly felt as wide as the age of the trees. When she was born, I had just graduated high school. I was on my gap year in Israel and doing the hostel Eurorail run when she was in kindergarten. When she was in prep, I was at university.

But I returned to the moment and how I felt with the woman in front of me. Even though I was nervous with giddy excitement, what struck me was how calm and relaxed I felt with her. We sat down on the grass and, inhaling nervously, I leaned over her. I looked at her face below me, angelic like in the movies, with the sun radiating between the trees. It couldn't have been better scripted. Our heads touched, but my glasses got in the way (fashionable round ones to dissemble the appearance of a professor, though the rest of my dress sense was my way of defying it). I pulled them off and reoriented myself. We kissed and I smiled. I wasn't sure how to read her smile back.

We returned to the car. I turned on the engine and looked in the rear-view mirror so I could safely manoeuvre the wheels over the rough terrain. My face was blurred.

'Shit. My glasses!'

'Where?'

'I've left them.'

We spent the next half-hour scouring the field like a game of manoeuvres at a youth movement camp, searching for my Belgian frames with their multifocal lenses. How could I not have noticed?

'I feel like we're in a Woody Allen movie,' Michelle said, crouching. Was that a good or a bad assessment? I wondered.

'Got them,' Michelle yelled. She held up my glasses.

I fished in my pocket for something to wipe them. All I had was a serviette. I cleaned the glasses and pressed them back against my face. I was the archetypal schlemiel, the clown, and in that moment I knew the Woody Allen comparison wasn't a good thing.

'What's that on your T-shirt?' she said.

'What?'

'You're bleeding.'

I jumped back. I let my jaw sink until I could see a trail of blood. It was flowing from my neck. I had to control myself. I couldn't allow myself to exhibit my exaggerated fear of spiders. Not only spiders, but any creepy-crawly. I put a finger to the trail, took the crumpled serviette and dabbed it on my finger to examine it. Was it tomato paste or blood? I sensed I had mysteriously leapt from a Woody Allen to a Charlie Chaplin movie.

It was definitely blood. We searched for the source.

'There's a leech on you,' Michelle said. 'It's best to leave it till it engorges itself.'

I wanted to jump out of my skin. Michelle sensed how petrified I was, so against her better judgement she plucked it off my flesh. I tried to stay calm but no matter how much I pressed, the blood wouldn't staunch.

It was getting late, too late for the climactic dinner I had planned at another winery. I drove along the winding road with one hand on the steering wheel, the other nervously on my wound. The blood trickled down my neck the entire way until we reached the main road.

We laughed all the way home at the mishaps of the day, the laughter disguising my fear that I had lost my one big chance of turning her perception of me around. I felt more than ever like Uncle Marky, an old widower, or worse, a baby in a stained bib.

Michelle is a complex character, I've learned, full of paradoxical traits. She could be described as shy, yet her friends know how easily she centres herself in a room with her charm and hilarious mimicry. She has an unshakeable sense of integrity and justice, a sensitive and instinctive way of reading people like a fortune teller. Beneath her gentle exterior lies a warrior with loyal and nurturing virtues.

On this night when I drove her home, I saw a part of her that was unfamiliar to me. I suddenly saw her as a woman in her fullness, which our past had eclipsed. As she stood before me, with a smile that had melted many suitors before me, her beauty gripped my throat.

I froze. I hadn't done this for decades. I was literally petrified, every part of me. Was it guilt? The trauma of loss that made it difficult to admit to my arduous passion? We stood outside my car, my every tremble a subtle gesture that I wished to enter her home. I fumbled.

The moment passed. My hand dropped from the door that I'd chivalrously—anachronistically—opened for her.

'It's been a long day,' she said, smiling, meeting my nervousness. 'We had a funny day. That leech is to blame.'

I'd lost my chance of shifting from an avuncular figure to a romantic partner. I went home alone, pondering but not understanding how I had let slip my opportunity to advance one step further towards the relationship I was seeking.

I wrote a message the next day as if nothing had happened.

Her response: 'Yesterday was nice, but I think we need some time and space.'

It was like she'd hung up on me in the middle of a phone call. There was finality in her tone.

I spent the day sulking in solitude. It was a hot day, a Sunday, and I sat outside on a deckchair, reading. I couldn't concentrate on the page and my thoughts kept drifting to the night before. It all made sense: the pause that she requested, her belief that all along it was my grief channelling those messages, that perhaps the age difference was more significant than we both had thought, and that we had not seriously discussed whether I was prepared to have children again.

I couldn't get her out of my mind. I had fallen for her. It would be foolhardy to suggest I was actually in love with her at that stage of discovery—but I imagined being in love again. I broke the silence some days later and to my surprise, she agreed to meet for coffee. I felt triumphant. I was sure we would continue laughing about the leech, and that we could resume exploring our relationship.

Another Big Date, perhaps, this time out of a Humphrey Bogart movie. Little did I know that she had prepared a speech in which she firmly and unequivocally told me that we should stop entertaining a romantic possibility between us. I had to get it through my head that we were at different stages of our lives, that she wanted children, a family, and she wasn't sure I was right for her. She wanted to remain friends if that was possible, but her message reverberated in my ear. Over, over, over.

She had come for that purpose, not to have a drink with me and, having delivered the message, she was ready to leave.

'Give me a chance,' I pleaded. Over and over and over.

I kept talking. We sat there for four hours. It started to get dark outside. I have no recollection of what I said, but from my depths, I knew I had to fight harder against her resistance. I found the words that slowly managed to open her heart, then open it more and more, so by the end of the night, Michelle surprised herself. We agreed to continue exploring the possibilities in our relationship.

Hallelujah!

Several years later, she would tell me that my finest and most dangerous quality was that I had a power with words, and a charisma that made the words even more convincing. Perhaps it was a characteristic learned from my parents, who had survived the war by chicanery rather than retreat. She said it was a quality that worked magic for me, but could be dangerous when misused.

Even later, when I complained about excruciating pain, I did so with a grin on my face. My way with words, she said without blaming me, might have saved our relationship but that grin proved fateful when it came to saving my life.

Hallelujah!

I felt so certain of my triumph that the next morning I gathered my children and revealed that I had begun 'dating' a woman. I must have qualified it: not dating, but seeing, interested in, opening up the possibility of pursuing someone. I put conditional tenses around it. I wanted to know how they felt. I kept talking. Clumsiness has a way of tripping over itself and digging a deeper hole. If by chance I were to date this person, would they give me their blessing?

'Michelle Lesh,' Sarah interrupted. 'You mentioned you went for a walk along the beach the other day. It's Michelle, for sure.'

They looked at me, one by one, their responses bemused.

'And how many times have you seen her?'

'Three or four,' I answered.

'And does she share the same enthusiasm as you?'

'Emm. Umm.'

'Of course, Dad,' they said, almost in unison. 'We want you to be happy, and at least she's nice and we can trust her.'

I noticed the tears well up in Rachel, my youngest. And, I added, stepping right into the crater-sized hole I'd dug for myself, this person, this hypothetical person whose name I wouldn't confirm, would want children. One, probably two. A family.

Rachel could no longer hold back her tears. She dashed out of the kitchen.

'How could you say that to your kids?' Michelle later said to me. 'We don't even know if this is actually going to go anywhere. We barely know each other.'

Nothing had happened. But I was convinced that something could. So I resorted to sharpening my weapon on WhatsApp. Words and words and words. Paragraphs and paragraphs and paragraphs. Long screeds that went on for weeks, in which we occasionally caught up face to face. Michelle would later say it wasn't only my words that won her over in the first instance, but also getting to know my inner self, a better version of me. A depth that was often masked by my demeanour, especially my grin.

Although our difference in age often came up in conversation, Michelle joked that I was even younger than her. It wasn't that I was fit from yoga, gym and jogging, but that I was young at heart. She delighted in the way I interacted with a younger generation through my academic life, and always kept up with the latest debates, books and TV series. She laughed out loud when she overheard me on the phone explaining to one of my kids the meaning of 'woke' and 'cancel culture'. I might have been a baby-boomer parent, but she could see that I would also be an active and engaged millennial parent to a new child.

I must have sensed what she was feeling and that I had to move beyond my missives to reverse the embarrassment of our date in the countryside. I had to throw away the notes, the CVs, the fears, the shackles, my clothes. I picked a hotel and we drove there on a rainy day. I ran inside and asked if they had a spare room. It was late afternoon and that same night I had to host a public work panel on the topic of refugees. And here I was, escaping my home, internally displaced. The receptionist gave me the key card with a suspicious look. I ran out and opened the passenger door. We ran inside like two giggling children.

And that's it. We made love and, after I'd hosted a packed audience in the university auditorium, we used the key card again.

The days and weeks that followed were dizzy with love and loving and lovemaking. Michelle had come to Melbourne for three months to see her family and to do research for her academic work. Instead, she became distracted by me. I became fully distracted by her. We couldn't remain apart, but Michelle wasn't ready for our relationship to be public knowledge. She wanted the space to explore if we could truly be a couple. Her natural propensity was to shun the limelight, especially in the closely bound Jewish community in which I was hardly anonymous. I had founded an egalitarian synagogue, established a Jewish local social justice organisation, run a Jewish studies centre, become a spokesperson on intergenerational Holocaust trauma. My picture had once filled the cover of *Australian Jewish News*. It was inevitable that the noise of gossip would crescendo when our relationship came to light.

My children's fears were allayed once I fully confirmed whom I was dating. They knew Michelle. They trusted her. Gabe teased me and asked if we'd 'canoodled'.

'Cute word,' Michelle said when I told her. 'Please don't talk about that stuff with your kids.'

I told her not to worry and that I'd responded by asking nonchalantly if that was a card game.

Rachel was more direct. She wanted to know if I'd said 'I love you' to Michelle. I blushed and avoided it. 'Has she said if she loves you?'

I meekly nodded.

'I can write you a reference,' she laughed.

What I didn't say is that I'd spent the past three months writing my own reference. There were so many ways I had found to say 'I love you' to Michelle, first through secret codes and acronyms which became saturated with overwhelming feelings and actions. I hadn't recognised myself when I looked in the mirror during my long period of torturous anguish. Now when I look in the mirror, I am transformed. I feel that a halo, woven from limitless love, protects us. I feel like I am living in a fairytale narrated by the transformation that love has inscribed upon our union.

6

THE TIMING of everything was also made more difficult by the launch in July of my book, *Thirty Days*, written in memory of Kerryn in the first month after her death. I'd spent the remainder of the year reshaping it, first at a writer's retreat in the south of Spain set in the mountainous slopes of the Sierra Nevada. By the time Michelle came to Australia, the cover design was laid out, with Kerryn's photograph set against the aerogramme letters we used to exchange. The cover line was generously written by Raimond Gaita, the famous Australian moral philosopher and author of the best-selling book *Romulus, My Father*. I had known Rai for many years, as someone who was married to a Jewish Israeli woman whose beauty and depth were recognisable at first glance, and who took a similar position to me on Israel–Palestine and politics generally. We used to meet on the occasional evening at a wine bar, where we chewed the bone on world affairs. In 2009, Rai had invited me to deliver a lecture in his popular Wednesday Lecture series, which was included in an anthology he edited titled *Gaza: Morality, Law and Politics*.

The invitation for Rai came from his long-time publishers. At the time, none of us realised that his stepdaughter Michelle—though he wouldn't use the word 'step', as she had grown up with him from the age of four—was someone I would be courting. That is not to say I wasn't aware of the relationship between Michelle and Rai, but no one could have foreseen that I would one day be pursuing his stepdaughter romantically.

We were offered the choice to remove Rai's words when our relationship was in its earliest stages. Michelle embraced the book, and even had a hand in its final edit, picking up errors or gently, maybe too gently, questioning whether I wanted to be so open about my marriage. Yet, publicity around the book created unavoidable tensions. The public me was projected as a grieving widower, and while I will always carry grief for Kerryn's death, the private me was at a new stage of regeneration built on my deepening love of Michelle. Rai's navigation of the dilemmas around his blurb on the book cover was typical of the nuanced and deeply thoughtful way he sliced through any issue with his razor-sharp mind—eschewing the lawnmower approach of either/or that characterised the degradation of much public discourse.

On matters of marriage, he was also an inspiration. One can understand the attraction that has sustained a model relationship of constant love by looking at early pictures of Michelle's mother, Yael. In these photos, Yael's bohemian Tel Aviv looks shine, and they continue now into her seventies, coupled with her elegance, wisdom and equanimity—qualities that make Michelle so similar to her.

Yael was first married to Isaac Lesh, who was born after the war and immigrated from Poland to Australia when he was just shy of thirteen. He studied at the cultural melting pot that was Elwood High, and then undertook a university degree in engineering before he developed a successful business selling high-end leather products. Indeed, he recalls with fondness how I came into one of his city stores under the Siricco chain, and how he helped choose a satchel for my university graduation. Michelle was only four years old! He and Yael had separated and three years later Isaac remarried, to Ann Hofman. She saw me in a jewellery shop while I was leaving to repair the wedding band that had been cut off my finger with hospital pliers ten months after Kerryn's death. Ann apparently returned home, not knowing I'd been pursuing her stepdaughter, and commented how pitifully skinny I still looked.

Michelle was born between these worlds. She speaks without qualification of a biological mother and father—Yael (Ima) and Isaac (Aba). But she refers to her mother and stepfather, Rai, and her father and stepmother, Ann—to all of them—as her parents. Two sets. She has many sisters. Dahlia is her elder sister from Yael and Isaac, and there are five more that she gained through the remarriages.

She grew up principally in Yael and Rai's home, where she stayed well into her late twenties. Her way of seeing the world, her ethical interest in politics and ideas, and her deep but critical connection to and love of Israel were nurtured by her upbringing with them and the nightly discussions at the dinner table. She also had a secure and loving place in Isaac and Ann's home, where she was enveloped in the warmth of large family meals, celebrations of Jewish festivals and milestones, and holidays by the sea and overseas. Their home was open, and Isaac's hospitable and naturally convivial character attracted Michelle and her friends to the house. I often think if it wasn't for the combination of her two upbringings—one in the seedy but later gentrified seaside area of St Kilda, the other in the leafy upper-class suburb of Toorak—that Michelle wouldn't be Michelle, and that I wouldn't have found a place of ease with her.

The family roots also extend to my parents, both Holocaust survivors and a generation older. It wasn't easy for Michelle to withstand my mother's interrogations and her probing questions about the relationships she'd had since Nadav. 'You see, I don't have time on my side,' my mother lamented. 'You are coming in when I'm old and I don't recognise myself.'

Michelle patiently indulged these speeches set among a shrine of photographs of the dead on the mantelpiece, empathising with my mother, even while feeling the sting of her judgement. I knew that over time my mother's refrain would shift from 'I want to love you' to 'I love you, I love you'.

My father, however, embraced Michelle from the outset, and recalled her grandfather Shmuel, with whom he was familiar through mutual friends. He also knew Isaac from the business world and family holidays when he took my mother around the back alleys of Bali for an entire day in search of quality sculptures for her home garden, based on his expertise as part owner of a Melbourne sculpture gallery. My father enlarged the most minute details he recalled about Michelle and would imitate how she had always worn her school jumper with her sleeves covering her hands.

Unsurprisingly, Johnny was one of the first people I talked to about my burgeoning relationship with Michelle. He was elated, for he had been one of my strongest emotional crutches and Michelle had a special place in his home. She knew more about the intricacies of his family life than I did, not only because of her bird's-eye position, but also her astute observational nous.

I still hold closely an image of Johnny at my son Gabe and Gabi's wedding, crying tears of laughter and sorrow as my parents, Yossl and Genia, danced to their anthem 'Rock Around the Clock'. That song is a beat that runs through their lives, first danced by my father alone when he came to Australia, about which he cheekily said that he went dancing eight times a week, 'tvice on Sunday'. Soon after my mother arrived, she caught his eye, and from that moment, they have rocked around the clock together, stepping in perfect harmony and knowing each other's movements like the inner mechanics of a Swiss watch. They danced to it twenty-five years ago at Station Pier, where their ships had docked in Australia, for the launch of my book about them; they've danced it at every simcha and at every Buchenwald Ball.

That night at Gabe and Gabi's wedding, I was too drunk to notice anything other than joyous celebration, oblivious to the fact that life was about to hit us with a second Jobian test.

REMARRIAGE

7

I WAS born under a white night sky shimmering with stars of ashen black. Each of the stars had a name, alien and almost unpronounceable, yet I learned through silent hints that my father had travelled to the one called Auschwitz, and that my mother had hidden in an unnamed hole dug into space. There were times when I would look up, especially on summer nights when the crickets chirruped a deafening song, and I saw that the sky had transformed into a translucent sheet of black, revealing the iridescent points of the great Southern Cross and a luminous kangaroo bounding through the galaxies. But in the darkness of my bedroom after the curtains had been drawn, I knew another night sky had returned and that my parents might be drifting there in their sleep.

My entire universe was populated by survivors, their tattooed numbers as natural as birthmarks, connected indecipherably to my own world of Jewish schools and kosher suburbs. On our biannual pilgrimages to Surfers Paradise, a northern eden of beaches that sweep the bottom of the world, virtually every lounge chair was occupied by a survivor, divided around the pool into tribal encampments—Poles, Hungarians, Czechs, Germans—ruled by the female sunworshippers who wore tin-foil breastplates over their bathers while the menfolk dozed or went for group walks along the beach. Yet even at this reunion of Jews from destroyed lands, the past seemed very far away. The only smoke in the hot blue sky came from their cigarettes, and the most urgent question was whose turn it was to deal the cards. Even when they traded memories, trumping each other with tales of narrow escapes and immeasurable loss, they hid their tears behind their sunglasses and went on to play the next round.

These survivors were known by the biblical term she'erit ha-peleita, 'the surviving remnant', and decades on, as most of them died a natural death one by one, my parents became remnants among the remnants. Yiddish was no longer the lingua franca of their haven, and the corridors of their apartment block were gradually populated by the children and grandchildren of their vanishing friends. For my parents, their paradise was now a place filled with memories of an erased world, one where they awaited their turn to earn a celestial plot.

For the duration of Kerryn's illness, and then for a year after, my parents prematurely stopped living. Their lives froze but were partly thawed by Gabe and Gabi's wedding. After the wedding, for the first time in almost two years, they allowed themselves to spend time in their apartment by the beach up north.

'Maybe it's time to come home,' I told them after several months.

'Yes, we're ready,' they answered, not realising that last leg of their trip was about to turn into hell.

What to say to these people whose entire existence revolved vicariously around the successes of their two sons? When my mother was asked about her idea of revenge for what she had suffered, her answer came back without hesitation, 'You, my children, are my revenge.'

How much to tell my parents about Johnny's condition? We gave them a diluted version of his cancer diagnosis. It was too much for their frail hearts to bear more information. Eventually, as Johnny began treatment, it was impossible to hide the truth. Johnny himself went to my parents and tried to soften the C word, but they heard, and their wails rose around them.

'This is worse than the camps,' lamented my father, who had been taken from his family at the age of twelve to work in a slave labour prison, before being sent to Auschwitz and Buchenwald. My mother agreed: it was the lowest point of their lives, whose nadir at the start was already beyond comprehension. 'I don't live,' she said, 'I exist.'

I had only just exited the kingdom of death as a carer and mourner. The door to a world of illness was held wide open for me again, and I walked through it, helping Johnny organise his personal and financial affairs, supporting him at medical appointments, though the brunt was carried by his wife, Anita, and five children. Like tumbling into Alice's rabbit hole,

I was back in a familiar place, one foot stuck in death, a hand reaching out to life and clinging to my new love, Michelle.

Johnny's cancer trajectory was different from Kerryn's. She had barely made it through the first round of chemotherapy and was sent to recover in a palliative care home. Johnny had the energy to do what he did best: use his charisma to gather people around him. He longed for companionship, could never be alone, always needed to schmooze. The chemo took, and he embarked with Anita on a trip to Israel, where they had lived for seven years and given birth to three of their five children.

Johnny's wellbeing gave us the signal that we could also travel. Michelle was keen to show me the landmarks of her life in Israel: the flower garden in the Habima theatre that chimed with classical music, the grungy streets of Florentin, the cafes she frequented, and the walk down the boulevards with their Bauhaus architecture. We also talked politics, about her earlier work at the human rights organisation B'Tselem, the period she slaved over a report known as the Turkel Commission which served as the basis internationally for military accountability, and, more recently, her job advising Israel's deputy attorney-general, a brilliant mind on the obligations of international law. He was admired and respected for his integrity internationally across the political spectrum. She expressed frustration at the lack of execution of her principles, but she was proud that she was contributing to eroding the oppression of Palestinians.

Israel was not just a workplace for Michelle; it was Yael's ancestral and familial home on her mother's side, which extended nine generations. Michelle showed me Yael's childhood apartment off the now trendy Rothschild Boulevard in Tel Aviv, and we travelled for lunches and dinners with both sides of her family, paternal and maternal. We also visited Michelle's father's cousin in the beach suburb of Bat Yam. She had survived the war hiding in the attic of a Polish family who were later recognised as Righteous Gentiles by Yad Vashem. After the war she was found and adopted by Isaac's newly married parents. She was sharp as a tack, but her husband was showing signs of dementia. Their brother-in-law was well known in Israel as the weightlifting trainer who had been killed during the Munich Olympics in 1972. Everyone we met had an exotic story but Isaac's cousin's bore an uncanny resemblance to my mother's: the way they were hidden during the war at the exact same age, and were adopted by relatives, in my mother's case by her aunt and uncle after my grandmother was killed in a car accident in Germany.

In Jerusalem I introduced Michelle to the world in which I had lived, first in 1986 after Oxford, and again in 1995 when my kids had gone to creche and kindergarten in their childhood version of a gap year. Michelle recalled visiting our home with Nadav during a year ten school trip, and reminded me of its details, down to the dark brown wallpaper in the kitchen. She was warmly embraced by my friends, and we reminisced about the student trip we had shared as we walked past the YMCA hotel where Michelle, Kerryn and I had sat together for breakfasts on the terrace beneath its arches, domes and tower.

The highlight of our visit was the wedding of Michelle's cousin, an occasion that gave me the opportunity to meet Yael's extended family. I knew she'd be self-conscious taking me, but her family was so warm and welcoming that those feelings of self-doubt dissipated quickly. Michelle tried to construct a family tree for me by pointing at everyone, saying this one is so-and-so's brother or sister, this one a nephew. It was impossible to keep up. Some had the name Meyuchas, which I understood from my semi-fluent Hebrew to mean 'privileged or esteemed'. In fact, it was their surname, which went back centuries, and there was even a synagogue in the Old City named for their family, who had arrived in Jerusalem after the Spanish Expulsion.

Yet there was something different about the connections Michelle drew around the web of family ties. Each person was simultaneously introduced in relation to a woman who had died. This one's daughter died at the age of thirty-nine from breast cancer, leaving behind a husband and three children under the age of six. This one's sister died at forty-six. Their mother, Michal, the great aunt after whom Michelle is named, had died at the same age. Michal's elder sister, Shoshana, Yael's mother and Michelle's grandmother, also died at forty-six, as did her mother. Forty-six is the oldest age of survival for those family members who had the gene and who developed breast or ovarian cancer, but who did not overcome it. That's as far back as they could trace the genetic tree, but it probably extends back centuries before the mutation had a name.

It made me realise how brave Michelle had been to undertake prophylactic surgery at an early age. Michelle and her sister, Dahlia, had themselves tested when they were twenty-nine and thirty-one respectively. Tails Michelle, heads Dahlia. Michelle sensed the news before it was broken by the way the genetic counsellor avoided eye contact with her when she walked into the room. Dahlia was in the clear; Michelle was a carrier.

'I'm safer than the rest of the population with my surgery,' she reminded me. But there was one caveat: the gene also caused ovarian cancer, one of the hidden and most deadly of cancers. Once it appeared, it would be too late. Michelle had been seeing a doctor who specialised in this area and monitored her.

'But how will he know when you need them removed?' I asked.

'The doctor says around forty.'

Michelle was thirty-seven. We had three years. Three years, we believed, before she would need to undergo a hysterectomy. It was a word I associated with older women. Women whose faces flushed in theatres. My mother had one at what I perceived to be an ancient age. It made Michelle feel more like my age. Yet I was healthy. My father had survived bowel cancer at ninety, and my intention was to live to that same age.

'I'm owed extra years,' I joked. I was fitter than ever, doing yoga, lifting weights. I also knew you're only as healthy as your next ailment. I was filled with self-confidence that I had my parents' genes of longevity. I hadn't begun my life in labour camps or hiding underground in the forests, malnourished. I had been spoiled, mollycoddled, always got what I wanted. And what I wanted was a long life, not cut short like Kerryn's, not awaiting the fate that was closing in on Johnny.

Dahlia, some years later, was diagnosed with breast cancer—the tragic irony of the sister who had felt so much guilt for testing negative on the BRCA test. It was the good luck bestowed by regular mammograms that Dahlia underwent because of the prevalent family history of cancer that found the adenocarcinoma deep within the breast tissue. Little did I know that when Dahlia's adenocarcinoma—a word previously unfamiliar to me—was detected in her, mine was already growing in me at a rapid pace.

By the time we returned home from Israel and a holiday in the Greek islands, we were questioning where home was. Our relationship had progressed dramatically, but we needed a common abode, a way out of the hide-and-seek between serviced apartments. Michelle had made a clear decision from the very beginning of our courtship that she would not stay at my family home out of respect for Kerryn. She never set foot in our bedroom.

I was typical of my circle of school friends, most of whom were born to at least one parent who was in Auschwitz, but atypical of diaspora Jews outside Australia. We all lived a block from where we grew up in Caulfield, and sent our kids to the same school we had attended for twelve years and on the same overseas study programs to Israel. It began to feel claustrophobic and I needed to break away. My haunt had been Carlisle Street, the stretch between the beach and the heartland of Jewish suburbia. I ate and shopped there, going on directly from there to work at university.

Seeing Yael and Rai's home in St Kilda rekindled my love for the beach, which I was already frequenting during regular jogs along the winding esplanade. Its streets were reminiscent of the black-and-white newsreels of my parents' youth, immigrant beach gatherings close to Port Melbourne—our Ellis Island, where they disembarked penniless in the postwar period, and where, back then, the *Spirit of Tasmania* anchored daily. I had gone to a synagogue in the adjacent suburb of

Elwood, where the rabbi had served as a chaplain in the British army and gave memorial sermons in Yiddish that breathed life into the spirit of his congregation of survivors. I had lived in a flat in Elwood, so my breakaway to St Kilda was more of a return to my roots.

I began searching in the area and quickly found the perfect home—at least perfect for me. Michelle, who didn't exactly see it as suitable for a family home, acknowledged the charms and benefits of the apartment with its rooftop overlooking Luna Park, the Palais Theatre and the bay, all icons to Melburnians and tourists.

I had always been fascinated by the Scenic Railway. As a child my father had taken me on the ride and just as it took off, I cried out loudly, 'Stop!', echoed by my father in his Yiddish accent, 'Shtop!', and we meekly slipped off. I know it's fanciful, but I imagine that I was shtopping the train less for my own cowardice than to protect my father from the memory of a train journey that had led to nowhere. The Palais also sticks in my mind for a protest rally against a tour of the Bolshoi Ballet Company in the 1970s, calling for the release of Refuseniks, Russian Jews imprisoned in the Soviet Union. Swaddled between these two buildings was a glimpse of the sea, and the sight of it filled me with a sense of freedom.

We purchased the apartment in the winter of 2017, while Johnny was still sick. Michelle returned from a holiday celebrating her father's seventieth birthday. Finally, we had a nest where we could live. While she was away, I had sorted the belongings in my Caulfield home of more than twenty years into piles: Charity, Storage, Children, Keep. I couriered lots of furniture and artwork and tchotchkes Kerryn and I had bought on our travels into the new apartment as a surprise for Michelle. I planted photographs of my family everywhere. Among them was a single photograph of me and Michelle from our holiday in Greece.

When she stepped into the apartment, I noticed her face freeze. I read it as a look of ebullient surprise and shock at what I'd achieved. She didn't say anything because she could see how excited I was by the work I'd put into preparing our new home. It was only when a friend of hers visited that the truth dawned on me.

'It's beautiful, but where is Michelle in all of this?' her friend asked. 'Tucked away in a little box somewhere?'

Despite my attempt to flee the heartland of the Melbourne Jewish shtetl, I had unknowingly built a replica of my previous home. How could I be so oblivious to Michelle's feelings? I had subtitled my book about Kerryn 'A Journey to the End of Love', a play on Leonard Cohen's song, but I was expressing something that bothered other bereaved spouses. They spoke about not being able to let go of the love they felt for their dead partners. I, too, continued to feel that kind of love for Kerryn, but I have always believed that some kinds of love—real love, I am tempted to say—requires two people: an opposite, a partner. Being *in* love certainly does. A dead person in a grave is not a partner. Michelle understood that the traumas of loss would always tug at me. She wasn't asking me to disappear Kerryn. On the contrary, she always encouraged me to check in on my children's feelings. She bought the memorial candles to make sure that Kerryn was present in our house. But she was right. It had to be our house that we created together.

8

AFTER A year of living in our home, I devised a plan for the perfect marriage proposal. I booked a table at Melbourne's iconic Stokehouse restaurant on the beach, where we had gone for dinner on the first anniversary of our union. It was the night we truly came together—physically, emotionally, denuded of restraint. A date I have kept on my calendar alongside our wedding anniversary.

Coincidentally, we were given the same table in the restaurant. The engagement ring was simple and elegant, inserted in a velvet box, inviting me to play the conventional role of the groom. I waited for dessert and fumbled under the table to open the box. It was stuck and Michelle looked at me, unaware of the surprise that awaited her. Once again, I had turned a romantic moment into a Woody Allen scene. Eventually, Michelle prised it open. She slid the ring onto her ring finger. I turned to the waiter and shared the news with him. He snapped a photograph of us, Michelle's hand resting on my shoulder, the ring sparkling.

We sent the photo out to family and friends and invited them to our place the following afternoon. In our mind, it would be a small affair, a way of mixing the families. No speeches. A modest spread.

True to character, Michelle, Yael, Dahlia and Ann sprang into action, preparing food and buying stacks of bagels and dips. By afternoon, the table was full, our apartment filled not only with family but also friends who dropped everything to celebrate with us. My kids mingled with all the guests, and I could see on their faces that they enjoyed sharing all that they were about to gain: a happy father who regarded himself as a role model to them in fulfilling a vow that over time we would be doubly happy; and a woman who would always be a confidante, a support, a key person in shaping their lives and central to our happiness. She was my wife-to-be, and our love for each other created unimaginable happiness for the two of us.

Our life before marriage was joyful and intense. It revolved around a combination of travel and career. A friend who saw us in London later remarked how happy and at one we were: 'I was very struck that I must have seen them at their happiest. I do remember one night in Soho thinking I had not seen Mark or Michelle carry themselves with such lightness. It was a joy to see them like that.'

Michelle was invited for consecutive years over July and August to teach an intensive course on International Criminal Law at the London School of Economics. I wouldn't take back those month-long sojourns over several summers for anything. We lived in an apartment in

Covent Garden, in the heart of the Seven Dials district. Michelle had to work hard to write her lectures, and her teaching schedule was gruelling as she oversaw a cohort of international students. It reminded me of my early years as an academic, when I was appointed as a lecturer at the University of Melbourne after completing my doctorate at Oxford. Every subject I taught was new, and I wrote each one word for word. Ten years later, I moved to Monash University and became director of the Australian Centre for Jewish Civilisation. Over the course of my career, teaching was a joy for me. I was always deeply grateful when, sometimes years later, students thanked me for the impact it had on their lives. I might have remained in my position at university, but I was sapped of energy by the double deal of cancer, and so left to pursue another dream of writing fiction. It was a dream that I had carried with me for decades, going back to my gap year in Israel, where I recall sitting in a Jerusalem forest reading Hermann Hesse's *Steppenwolf* and stumbling through Amos Oz's *My Michael* in the original Hebrew, a dictionary at hand. To this day, I wonder if letting go of my university career was a foolish gesture, a decision made in the thick of grief.

And so I spent my days in London distracted by the streets around me, always stopping at Neal's Yard for a porridge and indulgent cheese at a gourmet store. On weekends, we lazed in deck chairs in St James Park. At night we went out for dinner, focused on the

Ottolenghi-influenced restaurants which had proliferated across London. We took in a lot of theatre, which inspired me while I was working on my novel.

We set our wedding date for the summer of 2018, but an irresistible job opportunity arose for Michelle at the UN in Geneva, presenting us with a dilemma. She had secured the position as an investigator into alleged war crimes committed by Israel and Hamas during the border skirmishes, which took the lives of hundreds of Palestinians. The offer was too good to refuse, even if it meant relocating overseas and planning the wedding remotely. Not everyone welcomed it. Suspicion of the UN because of the recurrent hostility to Israel in many of its institutions, especially the Human Rights Council, is pervasive among Jews throughout the world. Some even believe that working for the Council amounts to treachery.

Michelle worked long hours and weekends on sections of the report outlining Israel's approach to accountability and on the instruments of international law most relevant to the facts on the ground as she saw them. Was it international humanitarian law or international human rights law or a creative adaptation of both? She was dismayed to discover that the answer had been assumed at the beginning of the inquiry rather than determined later by facts and jurisprudential reasoning. She was also disconcerted by the Commission of Inquiry's approach to the fact-finding and interviews. The working environment was under great pressure:

events were unfolding in real time, the team was small, deadlines were tight and the protagonists to the conflicts were uncooperative. The will to establish carefully the key factual basis of the protests, to identify all the parties involved and to establish the activities that fell within the Commission's mandate began to weaken.

In addition to disagreement about which instruments of law should apply, there was serious disagreement about whether to investigate the role that Hamas might be playing in the predominantly peaceful civilian demonstrations organised under the banner 'the Great March of Return'. Israel feared that, encouraged or manipulated by Hamas, thousands of protesters would storm the fence, break it down and stream into Israel. Yahya Sinwar, the military leader of Hamas, had referred to the protestors and the population of Gaza more generally as 'starving tigers', and clearly hoped that Hamas would ride the tiger into Israel if the opportunity presented itself. Were that to happen no one could seriously believe that Hamas or civilian demonstrators would then stage peaceful protests on the outskirts of Israeli communities close to the fence. Yet the response to Michelle's repeated insistence that it was an elementary obligation of a commission of inquiry into Israel's conduct to investigate whether Israel's claim, supported by reasonably credible evidence, was justified, perhaps even true, was at best half-hearted.

I supported her wholeheartedly. I shared her view of the Commission because I was familiar with her analysis of the Turkel Report which, in the aftermath of the

Gaza flotilla, highlighted the importance of the accountability mechanisms of international law. We spent many waking hours discussing the ethical and political aspects of a conflict that mattered deeply to both of us. I was proud of her integrity and courage even though it made things very hard for her and for our otherwise idyllic sojourn in the Swiss Alps. But above any intellectual reasons, I supported her because I love her.

We lived in Geneva for three winter months in an apartment with a view to Mont Blanc, on the edge of Lac Léman with its tall Jet d'Eau, dubbed the shpritz. It squirted water near the Bains des Pâquis, which was one of my favourite spots in Geneva. Located on the jetty, devoid of Swiss stuffiness, it had a restaurant with outdoor tables and benches where one could sit and grab a meal and glass of wine, as well as baths that become saunas over the winter months.

Our location in Geneva had special significance for me. After my father was liberated from Buchenwald, he was selected with a group of young boys, including his brother Boruch, to rehabilitate in Switzerland. My father lived for over a year in Geneva, and I used my time to peruse the archives, where I found records of the 'boys' from Buchenwald who were taught mechanical skills in Jewish-run training factories.

It also recalled a winter trip to Switzerland that I had taken in my childhood with my family and a coterie of friends, including one who would later become a significant doctor in my story. We went ice skating one day and my father, not one I imagined capable of sports, showed us how his dance moves could also slice ice, proving that he had once lived in this harsh climate. Indeed, when he arrived in Australia and started a modest clothing factory with Boruch, they called their nascent business Swiss Models, a title that sounds more suited to an escort agency than an ode to a period of their lives when they experienced freedom for the first time.

Living in the heart of Europe presented unforgettable opportunities. Paris was a short train ride away—only three hours to my favourite shop that specialised in a variety of chocolate mousse flavours, not to mention talks at the Shakespeare and Company bookshop and falafel in the Marais district. Or we could travel with friends by car in the opposite direction across the border into France and spend the day in the quaint town of Annecy, or for Michelle's birthday to a hotel above the clouds in Montreux, once home to Charlie Chaplin and Freddie Mercury, whose statue stands at the heart of this famous jazz city.

I returned home two weeks ahead of Michelle to prepare for our wedding. While I was food-tasting and checking out the song list with the band, Michelle was in Amman conducting interviews with Palestinians because her team wasn't given approval to enter Gaza. Two days after the wedding we returned to our stint in Geneva for what we expected to be two months. During that time, Michelle worked tirelessly but was often in conflict with the team. The tension and strain she was under began to take its toll. It soon became evident to us that ethically she had no option but to resign. In her eyes the Commission had failed to honour the trust of those who placed their faith in international law as a means to bring about a better world—faith that depended on their trust in its integrity. Hers was an act of conscience, true to her principles and to the dignity of international law.

She also had a more personal reason. Her disagreement with the Commission was not over its probable conclusions, but over its route to them. She knew that she would almost certainly agree with its justifiably severe judgments against Israel's conduct, and she knew that her support of those conclusions would be painful to her family in Israel. From the time she applied for a position with the Commission, she anticipated that would be likely and had been prepared to suffer their expressions of hurt and disapproval. But she was not prepared to do so on behalf of a Commission that had compromised itself in exactly the ways her relatives and many others who been had dismayed by the Human Rights Council's history believed that it would.

Michelle flew back for our wedding with only a few hectic days left for last-minute preparations. The wedding was held in Boneo on the Mornington Peninsula, set among Australian wildflowers that grew taller than head height, creating the impression of oneness with nature. Tents were pitched, a dance floor laid on the grass, a platform for the wedding canopy set overlooking the ocean, and fairy lights and lanterns hung outdoors among the casual seating. It was a summer day in December, but given the fickleness of Melbourne weather, all that was left to do was pray that the forecast of dark clouds wouldn't unleash a torrent of rain.

Our prayers were answered. The ceremony began with the immediate family arriving early for the traditional ritual of unveiling the bride, a practice that emulates the biblical story of Jacob checking that his chosen bride, Rachel, had not been substituted for her sister, Leah. It was impossible to hold back my tears as I unveiled Michelle. I was blown away by her beauty and my luck, though it was never only luck; it was persistence, an inner knowledge possessed by us both that we could have been made for each other. I felt privileged that she loved me and accepted my love in return. Against a sky that turned blue, I was led down to the canopy by my three kids, an act I will never take for granted, attested to by more of my tears.

We were fortunate that renowned musicians the Bashevis Singers agreed to play a Hebrew and Yiddish song we had chosen as we walked towards the canopy. The lyrics of the song 'Kol Galgal'—'The Sound of the Circle'—express the idea of the circle of life, or what Joni Mitchell calls 'the circle game' in her song of the same name. They started to sing them just as Michelle and I began the ceremony of encircling one another seven times, a number with mystical significance. Finally, came the climactic moment where the groom alone traditionally stamps on the glass, but in keeping with the deepest aspect of our relationship with each other, both Michelle and I each broke a glass under our feet.

The sound of glass crashing into tiny fragments carries with it the meaning that even in our happiest moment, the world is broken, and that our task is to repair it piece by piece, a call to social justice that underpins one of the core messages of Judaism—tikkun olam, 'healing the world'. The combination of elements under the canopy is carried deep in our unconscious as a rapturous moment that transcends rational description—the unified beauty of nature, family, music and that alchemic potion of grief, gratitude and boundless love.

The emotionally and spiritually profound tone of the wedding ceremony abruptly transformed into a party, with a band playing on a stage in a marquee and whipping all our guests into an airless and frenzied hora. Michelle and I were whizzed, spun, thrown, gripped like a totem, and held aloft on muscular shoulders or on wooden chairs. We reached out to hold hands, first with a kerchief, and then sweaty palm to sweaty palm. Friends formed a human corridor of crossed arms onto which we carelessly flung ourselves, trusting that we wouldn't fall between the cracks onto the ground. We bounced high in the air, our bodies twisting along the passageway of sturdy arms until we reached the end for one last final toss before landing perilously on safe ground. Energised by the atmosphere and alcohol,

I fell onto my knees and bowed to my goddess bride, and then the two of us—me in my suit, Michelle in her floor-length wedding drcss—shifted into a downward dog yoga pose to the applause of the crowd.

Just when we believed the atmosphere had reached its peak, my elderly parents took to the stage. My father, aged ninety, showed us his moves. It was as if time had frozen, and he was back in his youth. I can still hear him laughing at the front of the stage like a rock star. Our friends cried and marvelled at the sight, which was heightened when my mother took to the stage alongside him. It was a cue for the orchestra to play 'Rock Around the Clock'. Miraculously, their clock wound up again. Michelle and I, and her family and my children, joined in, but not one of us could dance with the verve and rhythm of these two lovebirds. Passion and mourning are the most potent mixture to stir the emotions, and ours spun until we were so dizzy that I recall flopping onto the dance floor, washed out in my pale blue suit, drenched in sweat.

'We did it for you,' my mother later said, 'because we love you and we love Michelle. We want you to be happy. You deserve it.'

We had decided against an emcee for the evening, preferring the casual atmosphere of select family members rising to speak on the podium. My three children stepped onto the dais and took the microphone. Michelle was in on the secret. The act itself, as much as the words, demonstrated that they had absorbed the message I had tried so hard to impart to them: we have to be doubly happy for Mum. I had found that double happiness in my own life, and they were publicly exhibiting that they shared in their own, and my, regeneration. As much as the pain of their loss persisted, they fully embraced me and Michelle soon after the beginnings of our relationship and now as a married couple. My happiness that night increased exponentially with every word they uttered, each in turn.

Then it was Michelle's turn. She spoke compassionately of the 'irrevocable void' in my children's lives and her regard for my 'positive and life-affirming attitude' which allows me to 'confront any challenge and hardship in a way that allows for renewal'.

Yet it was the final word in her speech that haunts me. One single word about the nature of our love: 'My love for him, and his for me, is palpable every minute of the day. And tonight, more so than ever, at a wedding that has grown from a relationship that sprang from unexpected beginnings to a connection that is so overwhelming, natural and forever.'

Forever.

The same sentiment was replicated by Rai with his profound words at the end of his thoughtful speech: 'Michelle and Mark, may you love each other so deeply that every day until you die you bless the moment you fell in love.'

While I always knew that the day I die would naturally come before Michelle's, I always believed that the length of my second marriage might surpass the duration of my first. It wasn't only because my children called me Benjamin Button in their speech. Despite my white hair, I was optimistic in believing that I would be dancing together with Michelle into my nineties. But even in a life of longevity for me, I would leave Michelle as a widow at the age of seventy. My guilt was pricked when I heard those words intended as a blessing—'every day until you die you bless the moment you fell in love' and 'forever'. I want to freeze time at the moment Michelle and I joined my parents in their dance on the stage, rocking around the clock.

9

JOHNNY NEVER made it to our wedding. When I spoke about him during my speech, the sun behind me in the open marquee was setting beyond the ocean, radiating an iridescent light that blinded the gathering, who audibly gasped as though it was my brother descending from the sky.

He died on Kerryn's birthday, ten months after his diagnosis. She had died ten months after hers on the eve of his birthday, and was buried the next day. The timing of their deaths created an eerie symmetry, yet their experiences were different. All Kerryn wanted was to be surrounded by family and friends. The kitchen was often full of visitors. I found it intrusive. I wanted to keep Kerryn all for myself. I was addicted to caring for her. I often left the room when visitors came, and holed up by myself in my bedroom, wallowing in self-pity. For me, the world was impenetrable.

Anything that belonged to the life of the living broke that cocoon of safety. Kerryn's authentic expression of herself was in giving people love. They couldn't get enough of her. She laughed boisterously as though she was healthy. She shopped for the kids while distributing clothes to her friends. She drove with me to the Yarra

Valley in search of wedding venues for Gabe's wedding, no matter her levels of fatigue. But she sensed she wouldn't be alive by the set date. Her mother had managed to be present at our wedding and at the birth of her first grandchild but died soon after.

'I can't fight so long,' Kerryn cried. 'I want to be there, but I don't have my mother's strength.'

I consoled her. 'It has nothing to do with strength. It's the cancer. It's not you.'

Johnny dealt with his ordeal differently. He was a larger-than-life character, the fabulous one whose charisma touched everyone. Like my father, he could connect the intricate leaves of a family tree and tell stories about each branch. He was a legendary orator, with a brilliant mind. Family meant everything, as did his engagement in community. When he was in Israel on his last holiday, he sat in the lounge of his hotel. By then, the cancer had begun to seep into his bones, causing him immense pain. He had walked onto the plane in Australia, and by the time he returned home he was on crutches. Ensconced in the lounge on the top floor, he entertained Israeli dignitaries, including the leader of the Labor Party. He invited them to speak in Melbourne, and his proudest moments were at public events in halls and at his home as host to these speakers. Friends arranged for a posthumous Australian honour.

He chose to die at home, with his family caring for him in his study, surrounded by his book collection. People flowed through the room, paying respects, and as his end approached a vigil assembled on the floor, singing his favourite songs to him. It was different to the private way I played songs to Kerryn through my phone.

Both faced death in ways that mirrored how they had lived. It was a lesson that would come back to me through a story that has since taken on an acutely resonant meaning for me. It tells of a rabbi, Reb Zusia, who lay weeping on his deathbed. His disciples were disbelieving. 'Why, our Rabbi, do you cry? You of all people will merit a place above all other places in heaven.'

The rabbi answered, 'I'm not afraid, my students, if when I meet the Holy One I am asked, Reb Zusia, why weren't you more like Abraham? And I'm not afraid if when I reach the gates I'm asked, Reb Zusia, why weren't you more like Moses?' He heaved his last breath after emitting these words. 'What I fear, is that when I face God, I will be asked, Reb Zusia, why weren't you Reb Zusia?'

I heard that story in school at a religious camp and loved it, though when I look back I had to rescue it from the way it had been presented to manipulate our emotions. Stripped of that context, the story carries with it something profound: it's impossible for us to understand what it means to confront death until we do. Anything less is a counterfeit of the experience. But the rabbi's most important lesson is that we go gentlest into the night if we can take stock of our life and say truthfully to ourselves, from the depths of our anguish, 'I have been my most authentic expression of myself.'

I never believed I would be compelled to answer the question so early in my years.

My father never got to contemplate his death. Michelle and I had seen him over summer in Surfers Paradise at their beach apartment. For Americans, the equivalent setting was the Borscht Belt in the Catskill Mountains, with its hotels like Grossinger's, where the image of adolescent innocence was like a scene from *Dirty Dancing*. In fact, my mother was once summoned to an apartment that had been overrun by blond surfies—or bodgies, as she called them—and in her accent sent them scampering with her scold: 'Zis place looks like a bressel.'

That Yiddish-inflected world has almost gone, replaced in part by the next generation and the grandchildren whose cheeks were perennially pinched in exhibitions of their successes. For my parents, it had become a lonely existence. The way my mother used to sing 'Those Were the Days' turned melancholy, accompanied by dramatic sighs. She spent her days smoking on the balcony overlooking the ocean, but hid her addiction when my father complained it would kill her. The evidence was there in the ashtray filled with dozens of cigarette butts. My father wandered through the downstairs arcade, hoping he might find a familiar face from the old days. Though he called his business daily, he had become increasingly less involved in its operations. He wandered the aisles in the basement Woolworths, or escaped into the dingy pokies rooms even though he had no interest in slot machines. He was embarrassed to be there when I called, and would answer, 'I'm valking on Cavill Avenue', not realising I could hear the ping of the machines from the main thoroughfare.

That was how he died. Late at night at the pokies, where he'd gone with my mother after dinner. He tripped in the dark on a step that has since been illuminated by OH&S stripes running along its length in order to warn people that they might fall. The records show the ambulance collected him from the entrance of the adjacent Beer Garden. Even in his pain, he managed to convince the ambulance drivers not to mention where they had found him. They transported him to hospital but had to wait, at my mother's insistence, for her to return to the apartment to collect his medications and presumably to tidy herself up.

When Michelle and I had spent time with them a month earlier, his stride had noticeably weakened, though his brain and humour were unscathed. He was known by everyone in restaurants and shops, and he had the habit of speaking to them in Yiddish as if they understood. His English was no less confusing. Once when he ordered 'raisin toast' for breakfast, his accent threw the waitress, who brought out two separate bowls of rice and toast.

As a father he was perfect in my eyes, idolised by all his grandchildren. Yossl wasn't just larger than life; he created a parallel world of human possibility, of kindness and of unconditional love. He was wise in business, always fair, and loved by everyone for his warmth, and for his recall of stories from fifty years ago. When he met someone Jewish he would pause, his mind whirred and an outpouring of memories associated with the person flowed down to details of who their grandmother had danced with at the Maison de Luxe in Elwood—often it was he himself—or how much per yard so-and-so's grandfather had paid for yarn. Nothing changed about him except the pace of his strides the night he tripped on an unlit step, and his lust for life, which had been shaken by the deaths of Kerryn and Johnny. Compared to my mother, he managed to escape the shrine of gilded memory in which she locked herself, and tried to find in his old age a life outside his mourning.

We got the phone call from Surfers the morning after his fall. He had told the nurses in hospital not to wake me at night. I was the only person he could call, having lost his eldest son. Within an hour, I was on a plane. When I arrived at the hospital, he was drugged out but recognised me. They were planning to operate on his broken hip. I was assured all was well. My mother lay on a stretcher bed beside him. His last words before he went into theatre were addressed to my mother in Yiddish. 'Shoyn gegessen? Have you eaten?'

I kissed my father good luck, and he went into surgery.

The news was good. The hip replacement was a success but it would take months of rehabilitation. I called home to Michelle and informed the others in the family that we might have to organise a roster in Surfers. Not long after, the doctors came and told me that they were concerned at how he was doing. He had internal bleeding and his organs were slowly shutting down. Within minutes, Michelle urged me to get my kids on the next flight. She joined as soon as she could the next morning.

As a family, we watched my father's decline. We held and kissed his hand.

'There's never been another Yossl,' my mother cried. She moaned and groaned that she didn't want to live without him. I was in the room when he took his last breath. It was the death he would have wanted: painless and unaware of his situation, like his friend Moishele, who happened to be the person who inspired Michelle's grandfather to immigrate to Australia, and who was an exemplar of a good death because he died of a heart attack in his sleep. My father, who had escaped death as a child, died by lottery in a gambling room at the age of ninety-two.

It took manoeuvrings with the help of the local rabbi to get my father to Melbourne, where he was mourned by hundreds. For me, his death heralded the end of an era. My mother claimed the title and role of matriarch but, struck a third time by grief, she became helpless. I was in effect responsible for her. I didn't want to be the patriarch but was left with no choice.

For my mother it proved to be the most traumatic of the three deaths. We had to introduce a team of carers to replace her one Yossl. She complained, 'I don't have a home. It's me and four walls. I talk to the dead and live with strangers who come in and out in shifts.'

She spent hours in her private courtyard, raking leaves, dragging statuettes while she cleaned around them and hiding the bruises and injuries from her falls. It was as if she wanted to fall, though we saw in her actions a continuation of behavioural patterns that stretched back decades: the way she would water the concrete pavement outside her house all the way to the street corner, or the doilies in her pantry cupboards upon which containers were lined in soldierly rows. My mother was compulsively driven by order but with the trilogy of deaths, her orderly world collapsed. The structure of things as they were meant to be played havoc with her mind, and her deafness left her locked inside a prison in which she heard a cacophony of sounds—songs she believed were sung at Kerryn's funeral, Johnny's oratory voice and conversations she had in Yiddish with my father, who had been her life's support. The arguments with her husband of seven decades were forgiven. Their marriage of seventy years was cast as a perfect union, where everything was shared, including grief. 'At least I had Yossl to mourn Kerryn and Johnny, but I don't have Yossl to mourn Yossl.'

She regressed further into her childhood, pulling out stories from the war I hadn't been able to extract when I wrote a book about the wartime suffering she and my father endured. The stories had a twisted fairytale quality to them, a once-upon-a-time aura that made my mother appear like someone who transcended her tales, a Red Riding Hood horror. The string of catastrophes that continued after the war that, from six years old, she had spent hidden underground by a Polish Catholic family—literally under the ground—could not correlate with anything one could imagine in this world. This was followed by the sequence of tragedies that began with accounts of her mother jumping off the train to Belzec, sometimes twice, sometimes thrice, which left me wondering if it was possible for anyone but a superhero to achieve these feats. But then, as though her fate was compelled to cut her down to a mere mortal, my mother's mother was killed at the end of the war in a vehicle collision when crossing the Polish–German border with her newborn, my mother's sister, Sylvia, on her lap.

The evidence of the car accident is in the burial spot of the grandmother I never knew in the former East Germany. I see it in the life of the baby, my Aunty Sylvia, who was salvaged and placed in a nursery where my grandfather found his new wife. He remained in Germany with his baby daughter, separating the sisters for ten years while my mother went ahead to Australia with my aunt and uncle, known to me in Polish as Ciociu and Wiociu, the couple I regarded as my proper grandparents.

For Michelle, taking on this trauma was a generous act of sacrifice. Pinned to the kitchen seat, she listened to my mother count the dead. Michelle never wanted to replace anyone. She wanted to help and nurture—her overriding quality—without expectation of anything in return. She shopped for groceries and meat for my mother regularly, visited her and got little thanks and recognition.

Slowly things began to change. 'I'm so happy to see my Markinu with someone, and with a good family,' my mother said repeatedly, and then turning to Michelle, she added the words that mattered: 'I love you.'

Nothing changed. Everything changed.

The burial plots we had bought were now filled with three people. My mother was desperate to join them.

RE-CREATION

10

IN THE cycle of Jewish ritual, the saddest of days commemorates the destruction of the Jerusalem Temple. Jews fast and sit on the floor in the posture of mourners, chanting from the Jeremiah Book of Lamentations. There is a verse in it that creates a parallel between grief and mourning with the weeping of Rachel, one of the biblical foremothers. Sung in a tune of inconsolable despair, the words of the psalmist capture the plight of the woman who cannot give birth to a child: 'A voice is heard in Ramah, weeping and great mourning, Rachel weeping and refusing to be comforted.' Rachel was twenty-two when she married Jacob, unable to bear children for fourteen years until the age of thirty-six.

Michelle was thirty-eight when she married me.

Our quest for a child was launched well before our marriage. Michelle had limited time before her ovaries had to be removed. But her yearning, like the biblical Rachel's, knew no bounds. It was a part of Michelle that I especially loved—the powerful maternal instinct. In this respect, she was her mother's daughter, as was Dahlia. It showed in the way she interacted as an aunt to Dahlia's children, acting as a role model to those children and revealing the kind of mother she would be.

After a year, it was time to consult a reproductive doctor. Michelle had already established a long relationship with a wonderful IVF specialist, Kate Stern, a leader in the field who wouldn't tolerate any funny business and combined a touch of the zany with extraordinary compassion and never-ending hope. Michelle first became a patient after she received her BRCA results; because of the risk of ovarian cancer, she was eligible to freeze her eggs. She began to do so from the age of thirty-two and continued for three years, by which time she had frozen over forty eggs.

There were many choices we had to make. Would we use her frozen eggs or fresh ones? Michelle and Kate wanted to start with fresh ones and preserve the younger ones in case the new ones didn't work, or for the possibility of a second child. The prospect of returning to those days of crying babies and twelve years of school meetings was overwhelming, yet there was no questioning the decision itself. I was in love with Michelle, and I would do it for her, and in doing it for her, I was doing it for us.

This inner conflict changed over time. I also yearned for a child and later, children, the more the possibility fell out of reach. I fantasised about the way children would keep me young, how I would turn my regular jogs on the beach into runs with a three-wheeler, the holidays we would take together, the books I would read to them, the gift of love they were, all the blessings to come. I knew the risks were increased at my age compared to when I had my first three children. My own sperm had different characteristics and Michelle's eggs, like all women, had begun their decline twenty years ago.

We began by undertaking genetic testing.

'Mine will be clear,' I said with a smug grin.

'It's not a competition,' she answered laughingly. 'I'm sure we'll both have issues. Everyone does once you start looking.'

The samples were tested and when the results came back, we both discovered we each had the rarest of recessive conditions. I might have expected some of the more common genetic mutations associated with Ashkenazi or European Jews, notably Tay-Sachs. There were mutations that deflated me, but none were shared between us so there was no danger of recessive complications.

The next question related to testing for the BRCA gene. There was a fifty per cent chance we would pass this on to a child. The risk of cancer was greater for a female. There were men in Michelle's family who had inherited the gene, and though none had developed cancer from it, they transmitted the gene to their daughters, for whom it posed a greater danger. We considered the morality of knowingly imposing something on a child with such high odds. On top of this, there was the difficulty of getting 'healthy' or workable embryos because genetic testing would significantly reduce the pool of viable embryos. The policy required all embryos with the identified gene to be discarded regardless of sex. We discussed it at length with a genetic counsellor, but we knew the answer in our hearts simply by looking at Michelle's experience. While the surgery had been traumatic for her, and clearly affected her life, she had more than managed. In twenty years' time when it might be an issue for our potential children, surely there would be medical advances.

From my perspective, Michelle's body was intact and beautiful. The scars were barely visible and so any physical qualms were totally absent for me. If the baby turned out to be BRCA positive, our relationship was an example that would be deepened through the crucible of our experience.

Then other questions followed on the consent forms. If we divorced, did I have the right to demand that any embryos be discarded? If I were to die, could she use them when we were no longer an us? Deeply in love, and believing in my invulnerability, I ticked these boxes nonchalantly, like they belonged to a world that we believed could never impact us. Our loving one another became intense, always passionate. Our lovemaking was deepened by the joyful desire to create the miracle of new life.

Anyone who has experienced IVF knows how onerous it is, primarily for the woman. The egg stimulation process, as distinct from preparation for implantation of an embryo, begins weeks ahead, with copious medications and daily injections and scans. Where many other women ask a family member or a friend to administer the injection, Michelle conducted everything herself, never complaining about the swelling and sometimes bruising around her waistline. There were numerous long drives for blood tests. Michelle's small veins didn't make her the ideal patient for the nurses who took blood, and she'd often leave with multiple failed attempts that turned into nasty-coloured bruises. She quickly learned to seek out a specific nurse who was able to draw her blood no matter how tricky her veins proved to be. She knew Michelle's arms so well that she had memorised the veins that weren't visible to the naked eye by reference to her freckles.

Once the precise time of ovulation arrived for retrieving eggs, we drove together to a clinic adjoining the hospital. Michelle was whisked away. Each round, Kate would hold Michelle's hand as the anaesthetic ran through her vein, making light banter about the latest novel she was reading until Michelle drifted off to sleep. Michelle would wake to a handwritten note from Kate that included a number. Sometimes the number augured positive news, such as ten or fifteen; at other times a figure that Michelle felt was a failure—five or three. Statistically, half of these eggs wouldn't survive, and of those that survived another half wouldn't make it to embryo stage.

Meanwhile, I was instructed to rush to a nearby building, where I alighted from a lift and reported to a receptionist. Sometimes I waited half an hour, depending on the time taken for the current occupants of the three booths to complete their job. I was finally led to a booth with a lock. The nurse provided a sanitary blue plastic sheet. There was a television set that didn't work but presumably in its heyday exhibited aids to stimulation. There was an adjacent bathroom and a couch. From thereon, it's a matter of finding a comfortable position and filling, mid-flow, a plastic bottle sealed with a yellow lid. There was nothing sensual to help this crucial ejaculation even though a life hinged on it. I felt tainted, because the environment conjured images of a sleazy movie booth in an old pornography cinema in Amsterdam.

I would bet that every male tilts the bottle to the side and ponders the same question. Is it enough? What of its viscosity? Another swirl, like swilling a vintage glass of wine. How motile are the swimmers? Furtively, the container is taken to the counter, weighed and matched to the man's name and address. I hope the nurse got it right, must be the common refrain of every male as he slips out of the lift into daylight, and waits to collect his wife or partner.

Each day is a waiting game. Who shall live and who shall die? How many eggs will survive day one? How many day five? Finally the day of implantation comes. Until COVID restrictions set in, I was allowed into the room. Our physical intimacy peaked at holding hands. The doctor emerged with a long tube that looked like a titillating wand, a magic one, we hoped. We were instructed to look at a monitor to witness the spiked spot that gradually moves down the fallopian tube like an amoeba until it lands—plop—into the uterus. In our eyes it was already beautiful. Our hopes were pinned on it becoming a human life.

Climax, without physical intimacy.

As Mary Poppins sings, 'In every job that must be done, there is an element of fun.'

Then comes the waiting game. The true test. Is she pregnant or not? The answer is ten days away.

On day ten, Michelle was out of the door from home early enough to beat peak-hour traffic, rushing to the other side of town to make sure the blood test was processed in time to receive the results by that same afternoon. The wait was excruciating, and Michelle could decipher the result by the tone of the nurse's voice who phoned with the news. I often wondered how she managed. There was the time she received the phone call with negative results and had to walk straight onto a stage to give an academic talk to a packed auditorium. Another time she received the call on the day she had to prepare a Passover feast in our home for sixty people and put on a brave face for our extended families while harbouring her grief. With each disappointment we kept the news private to avoid the pressures of being asked each time if it had worked.

Over the next three years, we experienced a series of failed attempts. The rhythm of our lives was synchronised to the mechanisms of IVF, physical and emotional. We had already undergone numerous cycles when the phone rang. It was the doctor's secretary, one of many, including the nurses, who fell into the orbit of people invested in the success of Michelle's pregnancy. She could barely contain herself. The news was positive. The hCG numbers that indicated signs of pregnancy were high—not quite as high as one might wish for—but not the zeroes we had been skirting. It was the first time in two years that we had received a positive result.

The second blood test showed a further increase in the hCG levels, again not to their optimal level, but high enough to cling to hope. The third test landed on the day Michelle turned forty, an event that would normally be an occasion for celebration. It was also the age at which her doctors had advised her to have her ovaries removed. Her family urged us to celebrate her birthday. Michelle understood their motives and was grateful but she was in no mood to celebrate. She had come to a milestone in her life drenched in sorrowful meaning: she was forty but without a child. Nonetheless she agreed, graciously. We chose a winery in Point Leo. The phone call came as entrées were being paraded out. This time the voice on the other end was forlorn. The numbers hadn't risen.

For Michelle, this was like a miscarriage. It *was* a miscarriage. She had carried a baby for a month but it had proved non-viable. On another occasion when the blood count gave us hope for five weeks, we watched as

Kate's instrument slid across Michelle's belly, searching for a heartbeat. She kept searching even when it was clear there was none. Michelle was required to undergo a suction procedure to remove the remaining tissue. The pathology results noted the gender of the foetus. Michelle wasn't prepared for this detail—for her, a personification of what we had lost—which deepened the pain.

Over this period, Michelle put on hold a book on which she had long been working. Kate was consulted about every career stint overseas. She contacted international colleagues in case we needed their care. The timing of our travel was synchronised with Michelle's cycles. She looked for jobs in international law outside of the academy. An underlying sadness hovered over her life. Often, she cried herself to sleep.

Kate's drawn face testified to how deeply she was affected by Michelle's sadness. Yet she persevered through every cycle with us. She responded to emails at 5 a.m. or 10 p.m. She did every test possible on Michelle's eggs and my sperm, but everything returned normal results. She began to move towards the more experimental side of things while still staying within the bounds of traditional medicine. We started using Michelle's younger eggs that had been frozen in her early thirties. We burned through them. The assumption was that it was a combination of bad luck, the inferior technology from the time Michelle froze her eggs, her current age and, it goes without saying, my age. Another hunch was that it was somehow related to the BRCA gene, though there was no evidence to prove this.

Kate started inserting two embryos at a time. It wasn't her medical preference, but we thought it was worth a shot. For me it was the perfect scenario: instant family, and then get on with life. Our family was replete with twins, including a pair born before the war to my maternal grandparents. Both died after birth, before my mother's only brother, after whom I am named, was murdered in Ukraine, the bloodlands of Nazi-occupied Europe.

Michelle's case was brought up in multidisciplinary meetings and a colleague was invited to reassess all the documentation. Perhaps a pair of fresh eyes would uncover something. The meeting was conducted on Zoom during Melbourne's first lockdown. We waited and waited for her colleague to appear. Finally, the doctor's face popped up on screen. 'I'm sorry I kept you waiting,' she began. 'I had no idea how big your file was and how long it would take to read through it.' She looked at us, her face strained and her eyes teary. 'You've done everything, Michelle,' she finally said. 'You've produced over one hundred eggs.'

Kate felt it was time to look elsewhere. She explained the statistics, that after so many attempts the chances of success drop. She was also worried about delaying the procedure to remove Michelle's ovaries. Michelle's other gynaecological specialist—Kate's colleague—had recommended the time had come to seriously consider removing them. I was open to anything that would ease the pain iconically represented by Rachel's lament. We toyed with the idea of a donor. To paraphrase the title of a famous children's book that I hoped we would one day read to our baby: 'We're going on an egg hunt.'

It's not so difficult to find sperm. The challenge is finding an egg. Most people travel overseas to IVF clinics to obtain a donor egg. In Victoria the alternative is to find an altruistic donor. We were warned against making deals under the table. Once cash was introduced, it would create complications. How would we find an altruistic donor? we asked.

'Advertise in the press,' Kate suggested. 'Preferably in rural areas; your chances for a younger donor will be increased.'

I was reluctant to follow the path of an unknown donor. One of Michelle's closest friends, Nat, was willing to donate. She had been by Michelle's side through her long IVF journey and wanted more than anything to help. One year younger than Michelle, Nat had completed her own family and was wondrously philosophical, practical and big-hearted about it. She wasn't the first to make an offer. Dahlia's generosity for her sister knew no bounds. She offered her own eggs and, if the doctor ruled that out because she was two years older than Michelle, then to be a surrogate, though she had already given birth to three children. Kate confirmed our hunch that she would not use eggs older than Michelle's. She explained that she did not believe the implantation was the problem, so surrogacy would not be required.

My daughter Sarah and her partner, Charlotte, also offered Charlotte's eggs. Charlotte explained her own roots and why it made the offer uncomplicated for her. She had been adopted within hours of her birth. Her adoptive mother—who she regarded as her 'mother' without qualification—went on to become a renowned haematologist in New Zealand, and subsequently adopted two more children from Russia. To this day, Charlotte is in close contact with her biological parents and their children. She tells us that hyphenated descriptors like 'step' and 'half' are too complicated for her. What's the problem with adding one more egg to the pie?

Michelle and I quickly came to the same conclusion: we could never ask this of Sarah, my own daughter, who was planning to be the child-bearing mother in her relationship with Charlotte. I had had to contort my head getting around the technical relationship it would produce but, that aside, my mission was to protect my daughter, not to complicate her life. We thanked Charlotte and Sarah for their heartfelt generosity, something we will never forget.

Once we accepted Nat's offer, there were so many factors to ponder. When would Nat tell her own children? Would it be public? Was it fair for others to know before our prospective child? Was I ready to look at a child who might in appearance carry half or all of the genes of a familiar face? We laughed that the child would grow up and refer to having a special relationship with Nat, like an aunty. Her husband, John, was on board. He was ready to be called anything as long as he could help.

Nat went ahead with an IVF cycle without fuss or drama in the midst of life with a job and three young kids. She respected our wish that she not tell anyone for the time being. It was characteristic of her that she never made us feel as though we had asked something huge of her. The cycle went smoothly, resulting in two embryos that we froze for when we thought we might need them.

Nonetheless, I remained concerned about Kate's hesitation over Nat's age. As the chances of pregnancy became slimmer, my reluctance to have an unknown donor declined. I became keen to explore the possibility of getting younger eggs as a backup option. In other circumstances that option would have been straightforward, but the government had prohibited travel because of COVID. Even if we were granted permission to go to LA and Barcelona, did we really want to enter a hot zone and risk catching the virus when it was peaking at its more virulent stages?

Still, we made an appointment with a partner doctor in an LA clinic. Over a computer screen, he explained the process in the US. He would do the work of the IVF doctor: that is, the egg retrieval and implanting of the embryo from the donor. The rest was up to a professional agency that transacted the sale of donor eggs. We were given a list of agencies with names such as Elevate, Growing Generations, A Perfect Match, all of which sounded like daytime television soap operas.

The dossiers on each person were detailed. Most were university students paying off their college loans at a price range of five to ten thousand dollars per egg. Some specialised in finding a Jewish match. My eyes immediately turned to one of the first pictures on a website specialising in college graduates, a beautiful blonde.

'I'm not so shallow,' I said to Michelle. What really attracted me was that she was musical and played violin in the college orchestra. The checklist of genetic conditions was clear. A detailed family tree was given, accompanied by a video of this blonde, I mean violinist, performing. To quote Yente in *Fiddler on the Roof*, 'It's a perfect match.'

'No, it's not,' Michelle interrupted my meanderings. 'I want someone who looks like me. Sorry you didn't find a blonde thirty-year-old to marry,' she laughed.

I took her cue and we studied more profiles. Some of them were fly-in donors from South America. But there was an abundance of choice of donor eggs from women in their twenties that were less likely than Nat's eggs to cause us the trauma of a miscarriage and more disappointment.

The choices were lined up: the embryos we had frozen with Nat's eggs, an overseas donor, an ad in a local rural newspaper. Adoption came up, but it seemed a distant option. Michelle wanted to experience the joy of carrying a child.

It left me wondering: would our marriage be marred if it were childless?

Kate called us into her rooms. 'It's been more than three years now,' she said. 'It's ultimately your choice, of course. But it's crunch time.' She felt she'd tried everything and was acutely aware that Michelle's ovaries needed to be removed. In her opinion it was time to move to donor eggs, but because Michelle was reluctant to stop trying with her own eggs, she was willing to do one more implantation with two of our remaining embryos.

Both of us had come to a point of exhaustion. In a discussion with Yael and Rai, we agonised over whether we should try one last time, risking the pain and grief that would follow failure. Michelle felt that if we didn't try, she would be forever haunted by the question of 'what if?' We agreed: one last try before going down the donor path.

For good measure, the embryos were implanted on our second wedding anniversary. It was the best present we could hope to receive. We couldn't even hold hands due to lockdowns. I waited outside the clinic in my car, watching through the screen of my phone.

Ten tense days. And then the call.

The hCG reading was promising.

We froze. Tears poured down Michelle's cheeks. We were even told the due date of the baby: 27 August

2021. The signs of pregnancy were there: the twenty-second embryo was alive and holding.

The next two days of waiting, we were balanced on a needle. Hoping against hope, thinking the worst. The reading from the blood test doubled. Still we didn't allow ourselves to believe that Michelle was pregnant. It must be an error. They'd mixed us up with someone else. Another three days. The numbers skyrocketed. We breathed heavily, excitedly. Our track record shows it won't survive. We waited anxiously for the five-week and then the seven-week scan.

Boom-boom. Boom-boom.

The faint echo of life in the heart chamber. More tears.

'You're officially pregnant, Michelle.'

After more than four years of yearning, and many more for Michelle, beginning long before she met me, her moment had arrived. With profound pleasure I witnessed her elation that our child was growing inside her. It felt miraculous. It *was* miraculous. We created a baby. We nourished our love and our future beckoned to us with glittering promises. The values and traditions we shared became more embodied in our lives because they were now realised in our baby and our love for it. I had consciously frozen a part of myself when grief struck me. I was excited to thaw it out.

Time to make an appointment with an obstetrician. We opted for Lionel Steinberg, aka Vaginal Lionel.

It was a nickname that stuck to him for his reputation for bucking the trend of opting for elective caesareans. I happened to have another relationship with him. As the former lay president of an orthodox progressive synagogue, I informally consecrated weddings and funerals. His son had married the daughter of one of my closest friends and the couple wanted me to conduct the wedding proceedings in a traditional but feminist style. So when we first entered his office and saw pictures of his first grandchild on his desk, I felt like part of the furniture.

Michelle also had a connection: Dahlia's three children had all been delivered by him. Lionel is known for his deadpan humour and his propensity to reel off statistics. It was obvious Lionel believed in vaginal births. 'Women have been doing it for thousands of years this way. But of course, it's your choice.'

Michelle didn't need convincing. Her preference had always been for a natural birth, a politically incorrect term that has been replaced by vaginal birth to avoid judgement of alternative choices. What bothered her was something that brought home that she was a carrier of the BRCA gene. Because of her mastectomy, she would be unable to breastfeed. She knew that colostrum was gold for a baby, as well as the benefits of breast milk. We investigated breast milk banks. Dahlia once again stepped in with a full heart. She volunteered to take Domperidone, a medication that would artificially induce milk. In the end we decided that Michelle would try the medication herself because she had heard of other cases of women who'd had mastectomies and released milk. We knew the chances were low and if Michelle were to produce milk, I'd be taking her straight to the doctor to examine why there was enough tissue left, perhaps vulnerable to cancer, to enable her to do it. Colostrum is gold, but life trumps everything.

We watched with bated breath the development of the baby from implantation to readiness to enter the world. But to adequately describe our emotions requires stronger, less clichéd, words from a thesaurus—trepidation, bafflement, fear, terror. Above all, disbelief and excitement, as we contemplated the progress of the pregnancy from its beginnings.

The first picture on the monitor: the embryo being inserted by test tube. It reminded me of the school films we watched that purported to teach us sex education through the life cycle of a kangaroo. The next scan showed a shadowy Rorschach image that developed into a Martian-shaped figure. A 13-week ultrasound highlighted a detailed image of a face squished against a placenta. We counted out loud, one, two, three, four, five fingers on each hand and five toes on each foot. It's possible the baby-in-waiting overheard because later, after leaving the womb, a favourite book delighted our child with these same words. We decide not to inquire about the sex of the baby.

I still carry an image of Michelle lying on the couch overcome with nausea, her stomach perched on a tower of pillows, satiating her cravings for salt with Savoy biscuits. And a comical picture of me assembling baby furniture that came boxed with lots of screws and bolts. In a short spate of time, I managed to construct a rocking chair from a manual and fix a formula dispenser that resembled a coffee machine. Michelle knighted me with a Hebrew label drawn from her days at youth movement camps: Rosh Techni, Head of the Technical Division.

I downloaded an app that shows the development of the baby in 3D. It illustrated the typical size of a baby relative to an animal or fruit. One week it was a peach or a puppy. In time, it would grow to a watermelon and lion. I could choose from different baby sketches to match our skin and appearance. The avatar baby grew each week, revealing new things it could do: breathe through its lungs, eat from the placenta on its own. I spun it around. I whizzed it to make Michelle nauseated, like a totem.

Before long, I didn't need to conjure our baby digitally. I could place my hand on Michelle's stomach and feel the exhilaration of our baby kicking and settling into different yogic positions.

To prepare for the actual birth, we enrolled in a class conducted by a passionate and energetic nurse in Lionel's rooms. I literally learned for the first time about the cervix and the stages of birth. It made the experience look like a round of world championship wrestling, especially when the nurse exhibited how the baby doll must push its way through a tiny canal. We were also shown a technique to manage pain using a rebozo, a stretchy Mexican scarf. An accompanying roar would also achieve the best result if it emanated from Michelle's low guttural palate, rather than at a high pitch. So much for the peaceful tranquillity of a darkened room; this was more like the jungle—the lion versus the pussy cat.

'I feel water leaking.'

'Your waters have broken. Quick, we have to leave.'

'No, it's too mild for that.'

'Call the hospital. That's what we're supposed to do.'

It was a Friday afternoon and Michelle was thirty-nine weeks pregnant. She scrambled for the phone and called the obstetrician's rooms. 'Hello, there's water leaking but I don't think they've broken.'

'It doesn't matter. You should come in at once to check.'

As instructed, we took the lift to the first floor of the hospital. Vaginal Lionel told us that the waters hadn't fully broken. It was what's called a hindwater leak, a description that sounds, if you excuse the parallel, like a dog taking a piss on a tree.

'Come back tomorrow,' he said. 'I'm giving you till Monday. If you don't go into spontaneous labour by then, you'll need a caesarean.'

We stared at each other.

Traitor. Caesarean Lionel.

He promised us a vaginal birth.

Michelle spent the weekend trying to self-induce. She rolled on blow-up balls and held her legs in the air. I massaged her pressure points. She drank raspberry tea and ate things that supposedly bring on labour. We went for long walks together, and when sleep evaded her, she sped up her step on a treadmill in the middle of the night.

On Saturday we packed. Michelle was already organised, but I still had my bags to fill. One with my clothes for the ward, another with clothes for the delivery suite, another with electronic equipment and two camera bags. Five bags just for me.

We loaded the car and threw everything over the baby seat that had already been fitted. How would we find room for the baby?

Doesn't matter. Worry about that after the baby is born.

We drove nervously to the hospital and Michelle turned on her meditation podcast. A female voice offered positive hypno-birthing affirmations.

Lionel did a vaginal examination. 'Come back tomorrow at the same time.'

We groaned and rolled our wheelies back to the car.

The ritual was repeated on Sunday morning. We reloaded the car and were sent home again. We had twenty-four hours till the deadline, or rather birthline. We decided not to cancel a pre-booked session on Zoom with a doula. The session was focused on how I, as a partner, could encourage Michelle through the pain. The session was enhanced by the presence of the doula's mother who was also a trained doula. Surprisingly, the doula and her mother pivoted, and gave tips about how I could position myself as a helper during a caesarean. Most importantly, I must ensure that I sequester the baby from the rapid steal of midwives to allow myself one-on-one skin-to-skin time. That was the catchword. It sounded mammalian, something primal, instinctive and essential for the survival of the baby.

We were then more confident of our readiness to face labour as a couple. We knew in the morning it would be C-Day. I ignored the inequitable distribution of luggage and salvaged my honour by refusing to allow Michelle to carry her one bag to the garage. It took two trips for me to juggle our luggage.

'Rosh Techni,' I boasted to Michelle.

'Dad joke,' she said.

'Fingers crossed,' I answered.

We laughed all the way to the birthing room.

11

I HAD expected a Balinese-style spa, with a pool of water in the middle, incense and dim candlelight. Instead, we found ourselves in a sanitised room with a hospital bed, bright fluorescent lights, laminated cupboards. What distinguished it from a normal ward was a blow-up ball. And to one side a baby's perspex bed with a blank hospital bracelet laid out on a rainbow-coloured blanket. All that was left to do was give birth and fill in the name on the bracelet.

We unpacked our essential belongings. I unloaded my stockpile of food and laid out the camera equipment. Two midwives dressed in blue gear and sanitised shower caps introduced themselves. Michelle was handed a hospital gown and undressed. She was hooked up to an IV on a tripod stand, our first introduction to medicalised labour. This was different to the photographs taped up on the walls during our birthing classes. The doctor arrived soon after. He explained that he was going to induce Michelle, give her till lunchtime and then do a vaginal examination to see how things were progressing.

For Michelle, it was an opportunity to give it one last shot. A roll and twirl on the blow-up ball. Other circus tricks that might encourage the baby out of its slumber inside the warm comfort of a sac of water. If I were the baby, I'd also be in no rush. Food on tap, familiar sounds of Mummy. No trauma.

Thinking of our baby in the womb reminded me of the time when I was influenced during my university years by Arthur Janov's book, *The Primal Scream.* Through my school days, I had suffered stomach pains, sharp stitches like daggers that immobilised me. I spent a disproportionate amount of time in what was known as Matron's Room. Perhaps I wanted to sleep during class, but the pain was real and acute enough to be sent home without any identifiable ailment. I had these pains as early as grade four because they prompted an operation to remove my appendix and fix a hernia, which left a deep physical scar on me. As a university student, I visited the one Janov practitioner I could find in the telephone directory. His house had an eerie, haunted feeling about it, illuminated only by candlelit sconces on the wall, and there was an upright piano which one imagined might be played by a skeleton.

It was a group class, and we were told by the gaunt psychiatrist to lie flat across the carpeted room. Then we were instructed to hyperventilate until we worked ourselves into a state of dizziness. At the count of three, we rose and acted as though we were crawling in the darkness through our mother's wombs. I was shocked at the reaction. People around me began to squeal like babies. They wailed as though they wanted to be breastfed. Were these people really feeling they were crawling out of a uterus, dilating an imaginary cervix along the way? Or was it like one of those hypnosis shows I'd gone to as a kid, where people mysteriously did crazy things at the command of a con artist who had presumably planted random actors in the audience?

I was sure that rebirthing would never work on me, but I was determined. I practised at home on the couch, lying and breathing heavily. Once my mother caught me. I think she thought I was lying in the dark executing a lewd act. I didn't have the balls to tell her the truth. It felt way more embarrassing to admit I was preparing to shoot myself through her aged vagina. The pains never went away until I married and left my family home for the first time. It would be a long time till I felt anything resembling them again, but by then it was too late to scream for Mummy.

In the relaxed atmosphere of the birthing room, far from the image I'd conjured in my mind, I snapped away with my camera. I took close-ups of Michelle's belly contracting, mild as the contractions still were. I focused my lens on the blank plastic bracelet, imagining the moment when the frame would be filled with our baby's name.

'Maybe you should move the car and validate the weekly pass,' Michelle said. 'While you have a chance.'

Neither of us wanted to admit I was a useless helper while we waited for C-time. 'Do you want some food?' I asked.

'No. But this is your last chance to fill up on supplies for yourself.'

We both knew what supplies meant. I snuck out of the hospital lockdown and told the guard I was moving my car. In fact, I walked further down the laneway to a trendy cafe, where I bought a delicious fresh salmon salad, a chocolate mousse to calm my fraying nerves and a latte.

As I was paying, my phone beeped. It was a message from Michelle: 'Lionel broke my waters. 4 cm dilated. Vaginal birth in next few hours!'

I looked this way and that. I remembered once being caught in an IRA bomb scare near Selfridges in Oxford Street. The bomb went off at the end of dinner. The police urged us to rush out, but the waiter chased us for the bill. Do I leave everything or pay?

I almost spilled the coffee on the way back. In the lobby on the ground floor, I bumped into Lionel returning to his rooms. I'm sure I could detect a proud grin behind his mask. Or was it me who was grinning?

'You better go up quickly,' he said. 'Your wife is going to give birth soon.'

I felt terrible for all my doubts. Most doctors would have insisted on a caesarean before the weekend. But Lionel held out for this possibility, knowing his trade so well.

When I got to the room the atmosphere had changed. There was no time for my camera. This was the time to put the doula instructions into action.

Michelle was smiling through the pain. 'Can you believe it?' She stumbled on her words. A contraction had started. It was way more intense than before I left the room.

'What can I do to help?' I asked Michelle.

'The TENS machine,' she said.

The TENS machine. Of course. We'd been trained in its use through a Zoom class and bad as I was at reading manuals, I made sure I studied how to use this indispensable device. If ever there was a time to rise to the occasion of Rosh Techni, it was now. It was the key to easing Michelle's pain. I opened the small briefcase and stuck two strips of electrified tape to her back. Next I positioned the kvetch—our word for a remote control—in her hand. The idea was to press hard and inflict electric shocks at the peak of each contraction as a distraction from the greater pain of the contractions.

Anyone who knows me and my professional work will guess where my mind wandered: the Stanley Milgram experiment, conducted in 1961, in which subjects were asked to inflict electric shocks on ordinary people in the name of science. The test of Nazi obedience, the measure of the fascist or authoritarian personality.

'Squeeze the handle,' I said, urging her to increase the pain threshold when I saw her face scrunch.

'This is great,' Michelle said. Then, suddenly, the contraption stopped working. She was pressing and pressing.

'Nothing's happening,' she said, frustrated.

'We have to dial up the pain level on the handle,' I said with an air of authority.

Her eyes clenched tightly; her teeth gnashed. She let out a light sound.

'Roar,' I said, 'Like a lion. Remember. From beneath your breath and press the handle.'

'The bloody machine isn't working,' she grunted. 'Check the batteries.'

I opened the contraption and checked. They were new batteries, but I changed them just in case. I squeezed the device between contractions.

'Do you feel anything?'

'Pain from my contractions. Nothing from the TENS.'

'That's impossible,' I answered, thinking that the machine should be renamed TENSE.

The next contraction swept over her.

'Fuck,' I said. 'What do we do?'

One of the nurses suggested I call the company. By the time I got through to the secretary in the TENS office, Michelle was roaring like an animal in the background.

'Your machine isn't working.'

'I'm sorry,' she said. 'We can get you a new one next time.'

Next time. Okay, I won't let my thoughts stray there. The banality of evil. The bureaucrat in disguise. On any other occasion, Michelle might have laughed with me. But not mid-roar.

I hung up the phone. I pleaded with the nurses.

'We might have a spare machine in a cupboard,' one of them said, as though it was contraband stash.

Within minutes my prayers had been answered. On behalf of Michelle, but also to save my own neck.

We refitted the strips. This time when Michelle squeezed, she felt its electric pulse radiate down her back.

'You see,' I said proudly. 'They gave us a faulty set. We'll sue the company per contraction.'

'RRRRRRRRRRRRRRR.'

She was now kneeling on all fours doing everything according to our preparations. Letting herself go. Breathing through the pain. Using the TENS machine for relief. For the next two hours she continued as the contractions intensified. I did have time for a thought to intrude, a beautiful one from Jewish mysticism. How when the world was created, God contracted her body which took up the entirety of existence in order to make space for the world. I didn't believe it literally. But soon, in this room, from a place of contraction, a real baby would emerge, a new world.

The midwives were now doing a lot of the work; I resumed my battle position as war photographer. I took photos of Michelle's face and had my camera at hand when Lionel was summonsed into the room.

'Didn't I tell you I wouldn't let you down?' he said in his South African accent.

'She's amazing,' I boasted, snapping a picture of Michelle.

The doctor told Michelle to turn on her side. He told me to grip one of her legs. I let go of my equipment so I could resume my rightful place on the front line.

'Now I'm going to ask you to breathe,' he instructed Michelle, 'and then when I say push, I want you to push with all your strength.'

Michelle, who I think of as frail as a bird, who when she runs flaps her arms like chicken wings, pushed harder than seemed humanly possible for her.

Nothing.

'We're going to do it again.' When she pushed this time, Lionel moved my arm to Michelle's opening. It was shuttered like a window with the head of the baby.

'Push,' Lionel said calmly. The head moved a bit, revealing its crown. The most fitting word for this majestic moment.

Knowing what to do with every move, with art as much as expertise, he pulled out one shoulder, instructed Michelle to breathe and pause, then to push again, pivoted the baby and pulled out the other one.

'Do you want to pull out your own baby?' Lionel asked Michelle.

She roared. He took it as consent.

He told her to lean forward with her arms, to reach for the baby emerging from within her, and to hold it.

'Push,' I hissed like revving a car.

In a magical moment neither of us will ever forget, Michelle gave it her everything. The head and the shoulders already out, then came a red torso, then two legs, all filled the void in the room with silence.

And then a cry.

'It's a girl.'

Her Majesty. The miracle of Embryo Number Twenty-two.

I know that what happened next happens every day to millions of people around the world, each according to the custom of their village or city. How can something so commonplace be so sublime, feel like the exemplar of uniqueness, generate the most rapturous feeling?

This was no time for dwelling on such things. We had reached the moment of one-on-one skin-on-skin time. First on Michelle, who cried as she caressed the baby at her breast. The baby instinctively took to her nipple. The nipple that couldn't yield nutritional sustenance, but latched, bonded, created that mysterious alchemy between a mother and her child.

My turn. I unzipped my hoodie and held the baby to my chest. The alchemy ran through me too. A font of love that wasn't in the world before, the bearing, in that revelatory instance, of the secret of the paradoxical uniqueness of birthing. This baby is mine. This baby is the world entire.

Lionel handed me a pair of gigantic scissors. He held up a huge piece of meat. Even though I'd been present at the birth of my three adult children, I was shocked by what I saw. The bloodiness of it. The toughness of the placenta. The butchery of cutting through the cord. Snap. The beginning of a journey. Dependent and autonomous. A biblical moment. Go forth.

In contrast to our expectation of the recovery from a caesarean, the hard work of a vaginal birth lasted just over two hours. Other than the TENS machine, Michelle didn't request or require anything else to help her: no drugs, no gas, no epidural, no stitches. As natural as you can get.

The baby was whisked away to be weighed, vaccinated with our consent, checked over. Meanwhile, Lionel pressed on Michelle's abdomen. Clots from a quick birth. Blood gushed out; their roles switched. The doctor was doing all the pushing, extracting what seemed to me to be frightening amounts of blood that spilt onto the floor. For Michelle, it was the most uncomfortable part of the birthing experience. A midwife placed a wet towel over her forehead. By the end, our sanitised room looked like an abattoir.

The baby lay peacefully and obediently on Michelle. I turned to Michelle and whispered, 'I'm glad it's a girl. She'll look after you if anything happens to me. Not that anything is going to happen. I'm going to live until a hundred for us.'

I sat beside Michelle, and imagined taking my baby to school, watching her graduate university, get married, close the circle and have a child of her own.

In these images, we remain frozen at our ages, forever young, though I am already sixty-one.

The next four days we hibernated with our unnamed baby in our ward. Over this time in hospital, we received instruction on how to swaddle a baby—or rather forty-nine different ways to swaddle a baby. We learned how to bathe a baby, wipe a baby's bottom and change her nappy, which since my first round of fatherhood had advanced to include a techno yellow stripe that faded into blue when the baby urinated. We learned forty-nine different ways of saying piss and shit, but settled on the Yiddishisms used by our parents, pish, kak, and for wind, pook or flotz.

Most of our effort went into feeding. We had no choice but to use formula, which in the hospital was provided ready-made in small bottles like those made for school lunch boxes. Michelle also wanted to try a method called supply-line feeding, which simulates the experience of breastfeeding. It's a complex procedure which none of the midwives on the ward had fully mastered and led to much spillage of milk. The idea was to tape a thin plastic tube to the bottle and hold it high to allow the milk to travel downward. The other end of the tube was taped to Michelle's nipple. Here, I admit to stepping in and taking a role once again as Rosh Techni—concentrating on the intricate task of taping the tube perfectly for this complex feat. I ended up teaching my technique to the lactation consults and even the salespeople from the company who provided the supply line.

Those first days we were exhausted from lack of sleep. I won't say the baby cried more often than an average one, but it still did what babies do. And in our hospital room, we co-co-slept edge-to-edge on a fold-out double bed, laid out as in that famous scene from a Marx Brothers movie where scores of people pile into a telephone booth. In any case, our physical needs didn't matter. I'm sure I kissed the baby on her keppeleh—the diminutive in Yiddish for head—at least a thousand, no, a hundred thousand times, to inhale the perfect aroma of a new life. There wasn't much hair to kiss but the outer layer of the skull was soft and unformed. One could rest one's lips on the crevice which would eventually join and harden.

These were precious days, days that would never return to us as each day we noticed a new development. Unlike other species, our baby was still totally dependent on us during her so-called fourth trimester. There is a Jewish saying about the task of perfecting the world that I learned to chant as a song: it's not for you to finish the work, but nor are you free to desist from starting. When it comes to a baby, however, there is no escape. The care is unrelenting and unending. No matter the hour, no matter your mood, you must finish the work the baby calls for in a subtle language a parent learns to decode—the movement of lips, a shriek, a startle.

'Isn't it time to name her?' Michelle asked on the third day.

'What's the rush?' I said. 'If it was a boy we'd be waiting till the eighth day of circumcision to name the baby.'

For some time, we'd been perusing the internet and a pile of books in search of a name that matched our cultural sensibilitics. Something Hebrew or biblical. We spent a day trying out our top-of-the-list names until we came to an agreement. Whatever name we chose, it would take time for the baby to grow into it. At the same time, we were aware that a name isn't a size 00 garment you changed after a couple of months.

We chose to announce our baby's birth by sending out a photograph to family and friends. On it was written our baby's name.

Melila Joni.

Melila, because we loved the mellifluous sound of it, and its meaning in Deuteronomy, which refers to the scattered sheaves of corn one leaves in one's field to be gathered by passers-by in need—just enough to fill a palm, no more, no less, so that no one goes hungry. (Melila rhymes with tequila, her philosopher-grandfather jokes as a mnemonic.) And Joni because it carried the sound of my father's name Joe, my late brother, Johnny, and the musical accompaniment of one of our favourite musicians, Joni Mitchell.

'It's perfect,' we said, kissing Melila Joni, or Lila for short, for the one hundred thousand and twenty-second time.

12

WE HAVE every day of Melila's life captured on film and video. There is the photograph of us leaving the hospital with me swinging her for the first time in a car capsule. There is the picture of Yael picking us up and filling her car with the excess luggage I had brought for my contribution to the hard toil of giving birth. Arriving at home in her—our—bedroom, once a private abode for us, now a tranquil space for co-sleeping, with Melila in her bassinet close to our bed.

There was no shortage of people who queued up to love Melila. But first among the first was the Queen Bee, my mother, who found a balm for her grief in the birth of our daughter. Her focus immediately fell on a ritual she has exercised on every one of her children, grandchildren and great-grandchildren. She insisted on being the first to wash their hair and scrub shampoo into their brains, ensuring their future brilliance. While she believed that the ritual worked, it didn't stop her ranking her clan according to her perception of their intelligence.

My mother would bathe the child exuberantly but confidently. She sang the Hebrew songs she had learned in displaced person camps to them, often boasting about her own brilliance and lamenting her lost opportunities, which she always blamed on the war. She also had this magical knack of calming a baby during the so-called witching hours. Aged eighty-seven, we trusted her to hold Melila and were enthralled by the way she chanted Yiddish incantations in a mesmerising lilt that belonged to a lost world. Melila, I realised, would be one of the youngest grandchildren of the world to be treated to these rituals from the shtetl, the small-town life of Jews in prewar Europe.

She would also be initiated into the family of Buchenwalders, survivors like my father who had been liberated from Buchenwald, the camp near Weimar. They had mostly been transported there at the end of the war from Auschwitz, but they all speak of their true birthdays—their rebirths—as falling on 11 April 1945, the day American soldiers entered the camp. There is an iconic photograph of 'The Boys', as they were called, gathered for a synagogue service in a wooden barrack of Buchenwald less than three months after the Nazis fled the camp. My father is seated near the front, an adolescent wearing a cap and looking straight into the eye of the camera, flanked two seats away by his brother. It is testimony to a legacy that grew, of affirming faith in life—if not in God, then in the humanity of the victims who were imprisoned in the pits of hell.

The Buchenwald Ball is one of the most oxymoronic concepts I've encountered and its purpose has always served as my guiding motto. Growing up, I never understood why my parents dressed in their finest clothes to go to the annual Buchenwald Ball. After secretly reading Elie Wiesel's *Night*, his account resembling my father's, I was haunted by its images and worried that my father was revisiting the camp where he had been interned. I had to wait till I was a young adult to be taken to one of these balls. I was shocked to enter a party room with balloons everywhere, Scotch flowing and wild dance. I learned then the most profound lesson that has been the legacy of Melbourne's Buchenwald Boys, a group that began as fifty-three men, with only six or so now remaining: you can dance in the shadows of your memories, affirm life as a moral response to death, build new worlds from the ashes of the old. My father believed he would be the last Buchenwalder in Australia. Now he has gone but our family are his surrogates, a new wing of the Buchenwald Ball clan, categorised by generations.

Melila. Lila. Lilush. Mimi. Miminu. Shnookie. Babaloonya. Angel from the Shamayim (Heaven). Zisseleh (sweet one). Choopchikonet. Pitzponet. Yaldonet. Ktantonet (a Hebrew limerick, Dr Seuss style).

These are some of the terms of endearment we use to describe our baby in permutations of English, Hebrew and Yiddish. Our kitchen has turned into a laboratory for her. Near the compulsory coffee machine, we have invested in a milk-dispensing machine. Press a button and instead of coffee, it measures out formula in grams and dispenses it into a bottle at the set temperature. Now a bottle isn't a bottle isn't a bottle. A diligent parent must find the perfect shape and size, and the perfect teat. Michelle invested a lot of her time in these choices. Then there is the sterilisation machine, in which we throw every item so it is clean for Babaloonya.

Then there are the slings of good fortune. I look online for the perfect one, imagining myself walking down the street with my baby tied to me. I order two different types and practise knotting them in front of a mirror. Finally, I'm ready to insert my baby. She snuggles her face against my chest. It's a dreamy feeling. I test the set-up by walking outside with her. She's so free compared to lying flat in a pram. I stop in front of a flower pot hanging from a fence and let her hands touch the petals. I'm in heaven. She's too small to reveal her feelings.

I stop at a traffic light. An old lady winks at me. 'Nothing like being with your grandchildren.'

The crossing changes from red to green. I linger behind, then catch up.

'It's my baby,' I protest, 'I'm the father.' The old woman overtakes me.

Everywhere I go, I get the thumbs up, 'Goodonya, Gramps', looking after the little one.

I learn to love the confusion. I will bamboozle them. I will always use humour as a weapon. I will carry my child as a weapon of my old–new youth. I will never grow old. I shall never wear the bottom of my trousers rolled—or maybe I will, given that fashion has changed since Prufrock.

But what of my child, what of Babaloonya Shnookie Lila Melila? What will she think when Gramps picks her up from school? Will she laugh? Or will she hide in the bushes until she's the last one left?

A nurse buzzes us into our two-week maternal healthcare appointment and weighs Melila. She's lost 0.25 grams. Judging by the look on the childcare expert's face, there is cause for alarm. She urges us to take Melila immediately to the Royal Children's Hospital Emergency Department. We race to the car and start driving.

'Are you sure we're doing the right thing?' Michelle asks. 'Maybe we should call the paediatrician.'

'We have no choice,' I say, and press hard on the pedal.

I am thinking of myself when I was a nine-month-old baby. I am coughing hoarsely. My father calls the doctor. He comes in with his briefcase and, according to the family mythology, hears another cough, packs his bag and tells my parents to watch for further signs of deterioration. The door clicks shut. I let out one more hoarse cough, like a messianic trumpet blast, almost as if to summon the doctor back. A knock on the door. My parents open it and the doctor rushes to my crib.

'This child has the croup. We have to get it to the hospital at once.'

My mother faints. My father grabs me and places me next to him in the car. He waves a white kerchief out of the window so he can speed and bypass traffic.

I arrive at the hospital, and I'm given an emergency tracheotomy, the scar of which remains on my throat. I'm in hospital for a week in an oxygen tent.

My mother meets the specialist doctor and throws herself onto the floor at his feet. 'Please, please, save my baby.'

I obviously recover to relay a tale I don't remember. Now, when my mother tells the story she has embellished it with one more item. She says that the source of her depression lies in the fear that I might have died. Not in her experience as a child hiding underground in darkness in the forest. Not in her elder brother being killed near Lodz in Poland on the way to Belzec. Not in the vehicle accident that killed her mother after the war when she was twelve years old. But her depression lies in me, an innocent baby. A cough.

Or is it a psychological inheritance?

I've tried out plenty of medications and, somehow, I've managed to defy the fall into depression, though I swing between poles in a manageable way. I exert a lot of effort in not being my mother's son.

To our good fortune, Melila never required the trip to the hospital. We went to the paediatrician's rooms instead. She examined her, reassured us that the weight loss was not a cause for concern, and told us to come back the following week to weigh her again.

It's hard settling on a name for your baby. It's also not so easy deciding on a titular name for yourself. Yael is known to everyone as Ima, Hebrew for mother. She is the iconic ima, a combination of nurturing warmth and selflessness. Should Michelle be Mum, Mummy or Ima? We decide on Ima. There will be two, but it feels comfortable.

As for me, should I form a pair with Michelle and call myself by the matching Hebrew appellation Aba, the name used by Michelle's father, even though he is a Polish immigrant? We decide that I will be Dad or Daddy, the way my kids address me, though sometimes they use the word 'tuts', a play on the Yiddish word 'tati'. We want Melila to feel one of four, to call her father by the same name as her elder siblings. We want to eliminate the hyphens of her being a half-sister.

When people talk to babies they often use third-person pronouns. I want to say Daddy is here but for some reason I keep calling myself Aba. And when I speak to Melila of her mother, I can't help but call Michelle Mummy. 'Mummy is preparing the bath and Aba will wash you.'

Michelle notices that I am doing the opposite of what we intended, creating a Mummy and Aba duo, rather than Ima and Daddy. I am also reverting to Yiddish words as though I'm my daughter's grandparent, such as zisseleh rather than the English equivalent, sweetness.

'Why are you calling yourself Aba?' Michelle asks, a tad confused.

I can't explain it but it keeps happening. The more I try to say 'Daddy', the word 'Aba' rolls off my tongue.

It feels like riding a bike, something ingrained, and then I remember that when they were young I wanted my three adult kids to call me Aba. It never stuck but the rhythm is there and I instinctively keep using it with Melila.

I'm embarrassed to admit to Michelle that I'm unconsciously rectifying history. That so much of what I am and will be to Melila is a reaction to, or an echo of, things I did with my three adult children. Some of it will be conscious. I have already resolved that I will never scream at Melila. I think back guiltily at all the times I yelled at my kids out of frustration. Sometimes the screaming was fierce, and in later conversations with them, they recall how frightened they felt. There were times when I smacked them.

Gabe, Sarah and Rachel instruct me on what not to do with Melila that I did with them, or to them.

'Don't do her homework for her,' Rachel says. I recall it being Kerryn who pushed me to do their school projects and write speeches for them.

'Be the parent that takes your kid to basketball games,' Sarah says.

'Don't make her religious or force her to wear a yarmulke,' they all laugh, recalling my zealous phase when we returned from a year away in Israel when they were young. I'm surprised how deeply they carry these memories.

I'm Rosh Reading when it comes to introducing Melila to children's literature. That night I choose *Where the Wild Things Are* and imagine I'm one of the animals.

I read the words in rhyme, sometimes substituting 'wild things' with the Yiddish word that stayed with Maurice Sendak from his childhood. Vilde Chaye. A drumbeat, primitive and coming from primordial forests. Vilde Chaye. It's a frightening book the way I am reading it. I swap it for *Peepo*. I look through the hole in the cover and make Melila laugh. She's less interested in the story than in playing by turning the pages.

'Tell Dadda what you see through the hole,' I say, consciously avoiding the appellation Aba.

I have so much history in me, I constantly fear it will slip out. One night I turn to Michelle in bed and call her Kerryn. She doesn't hear me. I curl up in a ball. My past. The way things once were. People die. But time is also a form of death. We just never stop to mourn it or else we'd be crying all the time.

Every month, we mark Melila's birthday anniversary by photographing her with wooden tiles that spell out her age. We stop to think how she has changed. First month. Crying. Feeding. Nappies. Crying. Feeding. Nappies. She graduates to smiles and laughing by the second month, then progresses to interacting with us. We love all of it, all of her, to bits. She's a chubby baby, with only a thin layer of hair. She looks like Rachel, people observe. And Rachel is a carbon copy of my mother.

My mother butts in, 'She's a Lesh. A Lesh. A copy of Michelle's father.'

'No,' I say, unwittingly drawn into her game, 'she looks like Rachel, which means she looks like you.'

'God forbid she looks like me,' my mother squeezes her wrinkled face. 'I can't even recognise myself. But when I was younger, people say I was a beauty.'

'That's Melila,' I say.

'A Lesh,' she hisses inexplicably.

By the next month my mother has changed her mind. 'She looks like my Markinu. She has his eyes. Bring me the photo on your mantelpiece of you and Johnny.' She stares at it. 'Yes, my dear.' And in the harmony of her favourite song, 'Those were the days, my son.'

Less than a month after Melila is born it is Rosh Hashanah, the Jewish New Year. My mother tells us she is frightened of being alone with carers. We decipher the hint and invite her to stay with us. Normally, we eat a lavish feast with a large family gathering but we're in the midst of another Melbourne lockdown. Michelle cooks a meal for twenty even though there are just three of us. I learn to boil Murray perch fish balls, the holiday dish of gefilte fish that my mother used to make. I've learned to make it in her style so that I can maintain the tradition when she is no longer with us.

Michelle sets the table with my mother's finest china, which can only be hand-washed. Surprisingly, it is my mother who compensates for the minuscule gathering by singing and rocking Melila to a mesmerising Yiddish chant that acts as a soporific for our baby.

My mother enjoys it so much that we pre-empt her desires by inviting her ten days later for Yom Kippur, the solemn day of repentance when we normally fast for twenty-four hours. It brings back powerful memories for me of sitting in synagogue with my father and Johnny, my mother in the women's gallery exhibiting her fashionable hat and attire.

Before the beginning of the fast my mother lights a memorial candle for her family who perished in the Holocaust. In recent years, she has added candles for Johnny and another for her husband. I light three candles: for Kerryn, Johnny and my father. The candles are a shrine of memory for the dead in my family. I take out my camera and snap a picture of Michelle holding Melila. My mother, however, is gazing at the candles, her eyes far away from the present—a granddaughter, and daughter-in-law who cares for her and tends to her needs—overpowered by the compulsion to count and mourn her losses.

Time flies. Lila's hair thickens to a dark colour with curls jutting out at the back.

'She's going to need a hair straightener,' Michelle laughs, holding a strand of her own long hair. 'She's got curly Jewish hair.'

Michelle too has changed. She speaks to Melila in the most animated voice, forming a bond that is a marvel to watch. She dances with our baby, speaks to her like a best friend on the telephone and can't hold back the laughter.

I wonder now if attachment can be split. I'm past pursuing my career ambitions and I work from home. At this stage of my life I have the luxury and good fortune to be hands-on and involved with caring for my baby. And yet I know that it is Michelle who is Melila's primary attachment. It is not just the division of hours that falls primarily on Michelle. I watch them together, both transforming and melding into one. It's expressed in the tiny things that add up to something more than I give.

Michelle is Rosh Everything when it comes to Melila. Nonetheless, she often says how happy it makes her and how it deepens our newly formed family life that I am so actively and joyously a father to Melila. Our happiness is obvious to everyone.

13

THE CIRCLE of love expands when ten weeks after Melila's birth she becomes a big aunty to twin boys of my daughter Sarah and her partner, Charlotte. The first-born is the smaller of the two: Miro Akiva, the middle name an ode to his maternal great-grandfather, an immigrant from Poland, who became a peddler in Broken Hill; followed by a thumping baby, Alva Lee, the middle name shared with his grandmother Kerryn.

We hereby declare the opening of the Baker family creche.

Ten weeks may separate Aunty Melila from her nephews Miro and Alva, but they lie on the same colourful mat, and sometimes Aunty paws the babies gently. We dream big dreams of the three of them growing up together. Already, the two elder sisters and big brother have bonded with Melila, but it is the babies that we hope will have each other's backs. We imagine holidays we will share, three mischievous kids out of a novel diving into waterholes and scavenging for treasured goods.

I become an expert juggler with the babies, finding a comfortable way of holding all three at once. I quickly realise I need another name for myself besides

Daddy. The decision is easy for me. I want to carry the European tradition of my father and call myself Zaida. As a joke, I dub myself Zaidad. Or in Hebrew, the combination of saba, meaning grandfather, and aba, meaning father, which together spell the slang word for 'all's cool'. Sababa.

What touches us most is when Sarah and Charlotte ask if Michelle will be the boys' savta, the Hebrew for grandmother, the name used for Yael by her grandchildren. Michelle laughs at first to be given a name with the elderly connotation of savta.

'I'm just getting my head around being an ima,' she says to me.

She is moved that Sarah and Charlotte see her in that light and have invited her to assume a privileged role. Nothing could ease Sarah's pain that her mother was not present when she gave birth, but I like to think that having Michelle there as a savta might have helped, though really it is as three new mothers that Michelle, Sarah and Charlotte have strengthened their bond.

When I reflect on my life at this point, the word I use is regeneration. I had promised Kerryn on her death bed that I wouldn't let the kids carry only the sadness of their loss but also bring them happiness. While we still grieve for her, we have fulfilled her promise with my motto, 'double happiness'. And it came to be that my wish was once again fulfilled when Gabe and Gabi announced their news that they were expecting a baby. From no babies months earlier, there are four born within a year, destined to be in the same year at school, growing up together and reaching their milestones together. How would Aunt Melila cope with so much responsibility? We naively believed nothing could break our happiness, whose blessings had quadrupled.

RETRIBUTION

14

WE WERE in a brief hiatus from one of Melbourne's many lockdowns when masks were torn off, al fresco restaurants overflowed in the summer heat, and the streets and shops thrummed with renewed vibrancy. I was partaking in the festivities mostly by taking Melila on permitted activities, for beach walks, splashing her feet in the water and introducing her to the world—seagulls, sand, fish and mainly dogs, the sight of which would soon elicit from Melila a mimetic 'woof'.

Beginning in December, I barely noticed the jolts of pain in my abdomen. I figured I'd eaten too much at dinner, or that there might be an ingredient like onion or garlic to which I was allergic. I'd always been prone to a sensitive stomach, bloating from certain foods that didn't agree with me. I'd tried different diets in the past and tested for coeliac disease.

'The Bakers have sensitive stomachs,' Michelle noted. Yet despite this, I ate unrestrained portions, particularly of pasta, which Michelle always fixed to perfection by peeling off the cherry tomato skins.

Michelle had been urging me to book in with a relevant medical specialist for a thorough examination. My earliest consultation about my abdominal bloating was at my regular GP clinic in mid-December when the pain was still tolerable. I was sent for a string of routine blood tests, an abdominal X-ray and CT scan. I managed to make an appointment at my regular scanning facility for the X-ray, but it was impossible to get a CT until after Christmas. I pressed for an appointment, fearful of the pressure on my stomach. Through persistence, I managed to get a cancellation at an associated clinic in the city.

The address in the CBD was located in an old historic building. Everything felt decrepit, from the smell of the corridors to the equipment, which looked like it had been borrowed from a 1950s Russian laboratory. I was injected with dye which emits a warm sensation that travels to your rectum. Then came the voice through the headphones: 'Breathe. Hold your breath. Continue breathing.' Because I was prepped by drinking several litres of water, I was desperate for the bathroom after the procedure. Even the porcelain-tiled urinal wall was historic, with steel bars on the base for standing on to protect your shoes from hapless leaks, and the smell of old urine mixed with fragrant yellow wash balls.

While I was relieving myself, my abdomen suddenly cramped, frightening me with its unexpected intensity. I limped out in a hunched position and told the technician who had administered the CT. He told me to lie down on a bed in the middle of a dark narrow corridor. The cramps continued until eventually they subsided. Part of me felt lucky; often when you go to a doctor your symptoms disappear. At least I'd be able to report and demonstrate the cause of my request for a CT scan.

A dithering radiologist appeared from behind a glass window and I relayed what had happened.

'I've looked at the scans,' he answered. 'I can assure you nothing is wrong.'

'But what about my cramps?' I protested.

Exhibit Number One: 'It's just the dye from the CT passing through your body. It will go away.'

I was left on the hospital bed until I was comfortable enough to leave on my own. I got home and barely mentioned the incident to Michelle.

A return visit to the GP that same week gave us an interpretation of the results of the CT scan. I told the doctor about the tight cramping and the radiologist's attribution of it to the injected dye.

Exhibit Number Two: 'Mark, the only thing wrong with you is that you're full of shit,' the doctor said with a chuckle.

What he meant was that the scan showed high faecal loading.

I left, worried that I'd be stranded by the medical fraternity over the summer break. I had one more option up my sleeve. I recalled that I'd recently received a letter in the mail reminding me of my biennial colonoscopy. I had ignored it to avoid going through the bowel preparation, but the pain in my stomach was intensifying, indicating something more concerning. I called the offices of the gastroenterologist and predictably was told that there was no appointment available until well after the break.

Hours later I received a call. It was from the gastroenterologist's wife and receptionist, who had always shown empathy to me after Kerryn's death. I recall us receiving the first warning of Kerryn's diagnosis with these words: 'The doctor would like you to return this evening to discuss your results.' Pause. 'And please bring your husband.'

I was on the gastroenterologist's frequent flier list, he liked to joke, so an appointment was opened up for me two days later.

I've done this numerous times before. The gown. Waiting, with daytime television muzak on a screen. I put on earphones to drown out the sound: Bach's *Cello Suites*. Finally, it was my turn. A brightly lit room. Human-shaped forms in masks and blue gowns from toe to head. The anaesthetist telling me about the procedure. The signing of consent forms. And then the appearance of the doctor. Light chatter.

Exhibit Number Three: 'I'm here for my regular colonoscopy but I've been having terrible abdominal pain. I need you to check if it's cancer.'

The word 'cancer' spluttered out for the first time, buried deep in my unconscious. I didn't believe it was cancer. That was impossible. Two young people in my family had already died; a third would be like a game I used to play when I was young: Go for Broke, the opposite of Monopoly, where the aim is to lose all your possessions. I had convinced myself that I was owed extra years. I promised Michelle repeatedly that I would live, like my father and my mother, till ninety. Melila would be thirty before I died. She might have to push me in a wheelchair to her wedding, but I'd be there.

Still, the feeling churning inside me brought out my fears, even if I meant it half-jokingly before the tranquillity brought upon me by the anaesthetic.

'I'm sure it's nothing,' the doctor answered.

A different voice. 'You'll just feel a small prick. Now count backwards from ten.'

I counted and fought the drowsiness until the fog of oblivion beat my resistance. A taste of death.

Someone tapped me. 'Where am I?'

'It's all done. Let's see if we can sit you up a bit.'

A dry mouth from the endoscopy and bloating added to my other worrying symptoms.

In between patients the doctor came up to my bed and leaned over.

Exhibit Number Four: 'You're all in the clear. A small cyst on your bowel we removed but that's nothing to worry about. You've had one before. We'll see you in two years.'

I called Michelle. In a slurred voice, I relayed the good news and added: 'Pity he didn't find anything to explain the pain.'

I avoided the word on the tip of my tongue. A tumour. A malignant one.

Over the next month, the pain and the bloating remained but didn't worsen. I managed to balance social activities and the joy of life with my baby while still searching for cures to the condition that was causing discomfort. I went to a physiotherapist because of a sore neck but asked if he could rub my stomach, which he took to be a strange request. I recall asking my hairdresser in banal banter if she had come across the symptoms I was experiencing. And I made repeated appointments with different GPs from the same practice, each of whom reviewed everything and added nothing new, other than a recommendation for more blood tests. The appointments were a mixture of in-room consultations and telehealth.

Exhibit Number Five: The GPs suggested it might be an allergy to some kind of food.

I tried to wean myself off wheat and lactose. I was often told by doctors that I needed to reduce, if not entirely stop, my caffeine intake but I wasn't willing to give up what for me is one of life's greatest pleasures. I have no other addictive vices, I pleaded; I don't smoke any substances and I only drink a glass or two of chardonnay a week. After Johnny died, I had switched from ordering a strong latte to a three-quarter latte, his favourite drink, so I could savour our times together. Most of all, I was looking forward to initiating Melila into my latte lifestyle. I imagined placing an order for her of one three-quarter babycino until I wouldn't even have to say it because the waiters at my latest coffee hole would know our needs when I arrived.

My coffee dreams were shattered when I tried saying 'one soy latte'. It didn't sound the same, and it certainly didn't taste the same. At home, I couldn't froth the latte smoothly and so I cheated with the coffee while Michelle went out of her way to cook us lactose- and gluten-free meals.

I decided to take it a step further. I'd heard about an app that tracked diet based on FODMAP. I read up about it; certain foods are high in ingredients that cause irritation to the digestive tract. There is no rhyme or logic to the foods, no way you can predict what appears on the list governed by a traffic light system: red, a big no; yellow, not too bad; and green, eat away. Blackberries are red; most cheeses surprisingly green; broccoli, thanks be to God, red; though unblessed be His name, broccolini stalks and heads snuck in as permissible. Some of the same foods are treated with inexplicable precision. Roma tomatoes are green, common raw tomatoes are yellow and cherry tomatoes, my favourite of course, are therefore a big fat round red dot.

I won't say I stuck to the rules like an orthodox Jew observes the law for fear of transgressing the Lord; I was more like a wishy-washy Jew, maintaining a strict kosher regime at home and eating more laxly in restaurants. For a time, I blamed the inflammations, as I called the syndrome of bloating and abdominal cramps, on either overeating or cheating.

Exhibit Number Six belongs to the wider category of consultations and the deterioration of the health system. By mid-January, the pain heightened, with the addition of severe backaches which I assumed was referred pain from my abdomen. I was complaining to everyone and being urged to book a consultation with the gastroenterologist who had conducted my colonoscopy. It was holiday time and, once again, everything was booked out. But my status as a past widower with a strong family history of cancer led to an intervention. The consultation was conducted by Zoom and the doctor appeared, slightly dishevelled. I didn't think at the time to question the limits of these telehealth calls when what was required was a thorough examination of my abdomen. Hands on, literally touching my stomach, for a patient that was complaining repeatedly about a worsening condition. This lackadaisical approach to medical care made it possible for doctors to substitute pastoral conversations for proper examinations and follow-up investigations until a diagnosis was made.

In this case, the doctor concluded that all I needed to do was take a different laxative. 'Mark, I understand why you feel this way. You've gone through a lot with so many losses. But I can assure you one hundred per cent this is not cancer. All the scans show that you're clear and I checked you carefully during the colonoscopy. Take a teaspoon once a day of fibre in a cup of water and in four months when we talk you'll be better.' One hundred per cent.

I was pretty pleased, as Larry David would say, and I quite liked the taste of the pebbles he'd suggested, which could be bought over the counter at a pharmacy. We were back to the 'you're full of shit' diagnosis. All that my pain required was a better laxative, which was promoted as such on the label: 'Because it works in your bowel not your stomach, there's no bloating. Because it works without bacterial breakdown, there's no gas to cause wind.'

I took the sweet pebbles assiduously, but the bloating, wind and pain only worsened. It would take a while, I assured myself.

Exhibit Number Seven, perhaps the most damning exhibit of all: I had lost several kilos. Over three months, six kilos to be precise, which eventually increased to a loss of nine. None of the doctors took this into account. I had started using the word 'pancreatitis' to diagnose myself and mentioned it to doctors I consulted. For some reason, my own diagnosis was ignored, and my condition treated as a case of constipation that would be cured by laxatives.

Ann and Rai had both suffered from episodes of pancreatitis. 'I've already asked about pancreatitis,' I said when they encouraged me to mention that condition. 'What about the pancreas in general?' Michelle said more than once, but every doctor assured me the source of pain was something else.

I believed the doctors. They were the professionals and I, a submissive patient, despite the second dissident opinion that spoke to me insistently from inside my gut.

Meanwhile, amid the onset of my pain, our attention turned to my mother, who contracted COVID.

For the previous two years, Michelle and I had been her primary external carers. My mother was helpless, having depended for everything on my father. He had followed her around with her tablets cupped in his hand. He was a social animal and would have gone out to dinners with friends, but he refused to leave my mother's side. He expressed his frustration at the way she obsessively cleaned the house. Her cleaning had become dangerous. She climbed ladders to reach hanging lamps, crawled under tables to polish silver bases. She had a regular housekeeper, but she cleaned the house before and after she arrived.

Her compulsiveness could be traced back to her younger years but appeared to be getting worse, along with other symptoms such as unfiltered verbosity. She never wore her hearing aids and mastered hiding her deafness by speechifying in the most dazzling, eloquent way. Was this just old age, the sign of someone locked in the four walls of her house and her head, silently counting the dead day and night?

It was clear she was deteriorating so we went in search of full-time care. We were lucky to find two Polish carers who were willing to share the load of sleeping over at night so she was covered 24/7. They each had their speciality. One was better at technology and could drive my mother to appointments. She also enjoyed watching 'golden oldies'. The other was a skilful cook who commandeered the television to watch Jamie Oliver shows.

My mother shrugged and said, 'What can I do? You can't expect everything in one person.'

Despite these limitations, the two carers brought a measure of security and solace to my mother, who enjoyed speaking her native language. Michelle and I visited most days, and stayed for Jamie-inspired dinners, trips to hearing-aid shops and kosher meat drop-offs.

There was only one hitch. We learned, at the peak of the pandemic, that both carers were anti-vaxxers. Even though they were responsible for the wellbeing of an elderly person, they refused to be vaccinated. We had no choice but to fire them. The timing couldn't have been more unfortunate. They left shortly after Melila was born, when Michelle and I were in the throes of our new euphoria. Our visits became less frequent. I often went alone and didn't stay long.

We searched for new carers but my mother had changed. She wanted to try sleeping alone. And she wanted more time to herself. We found substitute carers, but my mother's time alone was disastrous, as much as her desire to be more autonomous was admirable. She would fall into her rocky pond and bruise herself, requiring a string of medical appointments about which she repeated her refrain: 'I don't want to interfere in your life, my darling, but a son should take a mother to a doctor.'

Doctors.

On the days she was alone, she wouldn't put in her hearing aids, turn on the telephone or contact us.

The new carers annoyed her. One followed her around with a glass of water. A hilarious mimic, my mother imitated the meek way the carer would repeat robotically, 'Watah, watah.' The only liquid my mother drinks is Coke Zero. She developed a close relationship with one of the carers, a Polish hippie with tattoos on her toes who walked around barefoot and hugged my mother warmly.

When COVID hit my 87-year-old mother, Michelle and I were designated by the rules as close contacts because we'd been over all day during her contagious period before she tested positive. We were forced into isolation with a newborn baby. The Polish hippie carer volunteered, against our advice, to stay and look after my mother. We appreciated the gesture of care. My mother was taken to hospital on the second night after she became febrile and started hallucinating. She yelled at the nurses that she wanted to go home. Slowly she recovered but as she did, I began receiving awkward calls from the carer. She wept hysterically, complaining that my mother was impossible, and declared that she couldn't take it anymore. She had several times before acted in this way, and I had to convince her to stay. But sometimes she finished a shift early and always told us that she had to leave her car in my mother's garage because her frayed nerves required her to take a special spray which made her too drowsy to drive.

She abandoned my mother for good halfway through her recovery. Who can blame her? I thought. How wrong I was. It turned out that the carer was an alcoholic, and that the 'spray' was a bottle of whisky. My mother told us that whenever the carer chaperoned her in her car she dialled into a contraption. It was a compulsory breathalyser machine, highlighting the severity of her alcohol problem. I felt terrible for doubting my mother's instinctive suspicion of her, and for my bad judgement. After that, however, we struggled to find a suitable replacement, and my mother's grief deepened.

15

SO TOO did my pain deepen by the month and it felt like a car tyre had sprouted inside me and someone was pumping it up. I called myself the tin man because it felt that if someone knocked on my stomach or back I could have opened a steel door. My God, it's got to this and no one has ordered an MRI for me? I was alarmed by the weight I was losing. Something from the distant past resonated: the sharp stabbing pain in my belly from my schooldays. I called them stitches. For some inexplicable reason I associated them with a repetitive dream: I was lying in a bed that levitated and trembled. It might have been influenced by reading every Enid Blyton book ever written, one of my favourites being *The Wishing Chair* which sprouted wings and carried the children to faraway exotic lands. But there was nothing benevolent about the lands I journeyed through on my wishing bed. My dreams terrified me, as I continued flying until I felt I was an observer watching myself. Sometimes I woke screaming.

I had never really grown out of feeling like the child who escaped death, like my mother. One might say that my mother had experienced a perpetual death, stuck in darkness in a hole in the ground, her story a secret until I excavated it as an adult. I was always Markinu or Mocca, the diminutive for one who sucked his thumb, which I did till a late age, producing a blister that I called a rice bubble on my thumb. I was her pyezhki, onc who loves cuddles, a Krochmal, her maiden name, not a Baker. And I was sickly like her, curling up on her side of her bed, dinner served for me on a tray set before the television. She would prance around the bedroom sprinkling the freshly laundered bedsheets with eau de cologne, the smell of which has become my version of a Proustian madeleine.

Had the stabbing aches come back after a thirty-year respite? I needed an escape route from these pressures. A way to deflate the expanding tyre inside me. A way to understand myself.

Exhibit Number Eight: Me.

Somehow, I managed to juggle life while enduring the worsening pain. My focus remained on Melila, who was growing quickly. As each month passed, my mother insisted she looked more and more like Markinu. Her big brown eyes, her smile, her expressions—everything. The link to life that Melila restored to my mother was an antidote to her consuming grief. She needed to see her every day to lift her spirits, if not in real life, then on FaceTime through the video on the phone which, to our astonishment, she had mastered—most of the time.

'She is such a ganev [thief]. A heart ganev. I have two hearts because I have more love than fits into one. I could look at this child forever.' She said this often, meaning every word of it every time.

Melila was crawling around the house, nestling herself in the dishwasher and pulling out safety plugs that covered electricity outlets. My shift was at six in the morning. I slung my camera around my back and snapped the morning life of my neighbourhood while pushing Melila in an upright pram. We walked along the beachfront street and ended up at my favourite cafe on an outdoor table. I couldn't think of a better companion for breakfast. I ordered my regular, a three-quarter latte and poached eggs on toast, with smashed avocado for Melila. She smiled at the people around her. They got used to our regular presence and I made sure in casual conversation with strangers that they realised I was the father. A proud father.

Melila was an irresistible attraction. She developed the knack of making people laugh, as though she understood the timing of a comedian. She also responded with spontaneous pleasure to music, especially the Wiggles and 1970s Israeli classic children's songs. I swung her about while I belted out tunes from the *Sound of Music* or *Mary Poppins*, which transported me to an idealised version of my childhood, a place in heaven where there is nothing but pure love. No, it wasn't in heaven. It was in me and grew and swelled like a tidal wave.

At the same time, my mind was set on completing my stalled novel. All through January, the pain had dug into my stomach. I suggested to Michelle that I was onto my last chapter and felt sure that a week of isolation would help me finish the book. My life had become consumed by Melila, my mother and my preoccupation with my stomachache. The need to complete the novel weighed heavily on me. While Michelle attended a conference at her university, I had taken on the lion's share of care of Melila for a couple of days, hardly noteworthy of a mention in the Book of Martyrology compared to the daily responsibility Michelle carried. A week's break was too long to be away from Michelle and Melila. I would miss them too much, so four days only.

I searched the internet and that night, with Michelle's help and encouragement, I booked accommodation. It was early February, the peak of summer holidays. The main thing I needed to pack was my computer. It was the first time I'd been away from Melila and I missed everything about her, cries included. Michelle, in her true nurturing form, packed gourmet frozen dinners for every night. On the first night I ate a delicious eggplant parmigiana. The pain struck.

'Fuck food restrictions,' I thought. 'If it's not working, I'd rather the pain than the restraint.'

My accommodation was a gorgeous cottage near the hot springs of Hepburn. I sat and wrote on the balcony, listening to the birds as they swooped through the mountainous air. At dusk, a glass of wine in my hand and computer balanced on my lap, the cockatoos gathered and soared past the terrace, forcing me to duck in terror as though I was in a Hitchcock movie. I drove each day to the nearby town of Daylesford, a hipster enclave to a large queer population. I happened to notice a property for sale off a dirt-track road ten minutes from the town. I booked an inspection and immediately I knew I wanted this place for my modern blended family. I fantasised about the many weekends away, the children growing up as adolescents together among the kangaroos, summers diving into the dam and avoiding the yabbies that were known, at least by myth, to target a male's testicles.

A few weeks later, I drove back for the day with Michelle and Melila to inspect the property. Michelle felt the same about the place, and I presume Melila approved of her future lifestyle. We considered the proposition for some time, wavered with pros and cons. How would this city boy, afraid of spiders and snakes—afraid of nature—manage a property if I could barely manage myself, especially since The Pain had started?

Still, I had dreams of reinventing myself, of working the land among the dense, bare, fire-prone forests. I was also strongly influenced by my stepfather-in-law. After Rai had written his celebrated book, *Romulus, My Father*, he and Yael had bought a large tract of land in Romulus territory, close to the town of Maldon, between Castlemaine and Bendigo. They named it Shalvah, a Hebrew word meaning 'tranquillity'. And tranquil it was.

We had spent a few nights at their house that summer, some weeks before my solo writing retreat. The straw-bale house is powered by solar energy, augmented when necessart by a generator. The land has a harsh beauty and is home to mobs of kangaroos by day and night. Four or five old wattle trees on the property had died, leaving the twisted shapes of tree limbs among the rocks and boulders, some of which had Aboriginal significance, including a cave that one of Rai's Indigenous friends suspected was once used as a place for giving birth. Rai's book-lined study overlooked the dry land through a large round window, with a view across the plain to the blue Pyrenees. Yael tended to her garden patch and helped Rai care for the property. She planted as many of the seven fruits of the Bible that would grow there and be consistent with the native landscape—pomegranates, olives and the juiciest, sweetest figs which she often brought home to Melbourne as treats for us. A neighbouring farmer planted wheat and barley.

Early in the morning and at dusk I would go out and photograph the kangaroos, pushing the boundaries of safety by trying to get as close as possible. Rai took me to different areas to photograph; the more I snapped away, the more I became enchanted by the harsh landscape. At night we sat together for dinner indoors, or if it was warm enough outside on the verandah, and talked about politics and philosophy. I comfortably engaged him in table banter that lasted deep into the night, after the silhouette of the last kangaroo had hopped away. Rai would insist on leaving the lights off so we could experience inside and outside the changing colours of the darkening sky, which was a sublime idea but a sloppy way of finishing a meal.

We lamented the decline of universities, the cultural wars and the lack of nuance in contemporary discourse.

We talked about COVID, and the shallowness of reducing life to a mathematical calculus. We joked that we would join Extinction Rebellion and glue ourselves to the road at a street intersection. One of Rai's most cherished topics was about land, his attachment to it and, partly because of this, the relations between Australia's Indigenous and non-Indigenous peoples. His sense of who he is as a person, philosopher and writer has been deeply influenced by his boyhood in the farmlands of Central Victoria and his return to them when he was almost sixty.

Michelle and I also shared similar views on Israel–Palestine as Rai and Yael. We spoke of our despair, yet nitpicked every aspect of Israeli politics. After living with Yael for forty years, Rai had entered fully into her Jewish life, and was considered by family and many members of the community as an honorary Jew. Yael and I bonded over our love of the Hebrew language and literature and biblical stories. We shared an interest in the roots of words, their meanings and origins, and often exchanged fun facts and information about Jewish history. Yael had also recently taken an emotional interest in her Polish roots, and visited her father's birthplace with Rai, tracing the route of her father's escape from wartime Poland where he joined Anders' Army and later the Israeli Haganah.

Going back to my Daylesford dreams, I know that I was imagining Michelle and me cultivating our own tract of land in between writing. Michelle would grow a garden patch of her own, and I would mow the weeds on a tractor, steering between the menacing cacti. But I was no Rai, who had grown up tough, didn't squeal when he saw a huntsman spider and knew how to work machinery. Being Rosh Techni at home was a far cry from being able to care for the harsh, rocky land of Central Victoria, unforgiving to those who neglected it.

My kids were enthusiastic about the idea of a holiday house where we could spend summers and weekends, creating a future together. I took this as an embrace of our 'double happiness' philosophy. But we decided against purchasing the property. Practical reasons spoke too forcefully against it and we were all becoming ever more concerned over my inexplicable pain.

Once home from Daylesford there was a gap of only three days before embarking on a family holiday to the seaside peninsula town of Mount Martha. It was late February, the first time we'd be going away with Melila, my grandchildren and mother. I lay awake tossing from the pain, worried about how I'd manage. Another delay wasn't possible. Not for the first time, I made an appointment online after midnight to see a GP the next morning.

Michelle was relieved. We hoped this GP would pursue further investigation or take a more proactive diagnostic approach. I couldn't risk leaving for a holiday without one more opinion. Every single doctor proffered the same advice. The scans are clear. Why don't you try this laxative? I meekly accepted the consensual diagnosis but my gut, literally, would not allow me to escape the insistent fear that more was happening.

That morning hours before we departed for Mount Martha the doctor added one extra piece of advice: a referral to a gastroenterologist who specialised in the mind–gut connection.

'There's so much writing on it,' she said, and specifically recommended the bestselling book *Gut* by Giulia Enders. I was sure that it, finally, contained the answer to my problem if only I could find the right page. But it was too hard to read through the pain, so I downloaded it as an audiobook, something I had always regarded with a large dollop of snobbery as something other than reading.

My fears that the pain would inhibit my participation in holiday activities came to fruition. I spent much of the time in the bathroom, while through the door I could hear the raucous laughter of my family. Then came the news that blighted our holiday.

We couldn't keep it from my mother. Her sister, Sylvia, the baby who had been in the car accident with their mother—the grandmother I never knew—at the end of the war and survived, had also been experiencing stomach pain. She suffered many digestive ailments but this time, after a stint in hospital, the doctors discovered she had pancreatic cancer. They had already begun treating her with radiotherapy. The family was hopeful because the tumour had been detected so early.

My mother knew something was wrong at home, so we felt compelled to tell her. As a consequence, she spent much of the holiday outside, puffing away on a cigarette, grieving over her younger sister and bewailing the fate of the family. To her, it seemed that the adult sector of the family was being lopped off, leaving her as the lone survivor, like the little girl who was the only Jewish child from her Ukrainian shtetl to survive the war.

Her survival had always been a source of guilt because it was made possible by secondary guilt: her father had served on the Judenrat, the Jewish councils installed by the occupying Nazi forces to do the proxy work of 'administering' the Jewish population, who in most of the small towns of my mother's region numbered about half the population. On the day the Nazis liquidated her village, they gathered all the Jews in a valley and then transported them by train to the death-camp of Belzec. You could count the number of Jews who survived Belzec on one hand. My mother owes her own survival to preparations my grandfather made, possibly with foreknowledge of the fate of his Jewish neighbours, telling my mother to run to the forests where a family had been bribed to hide her. Added to the trauma of being hidden in a dark hole in the ground was the question, 'Am I the privileged one?' She must have always known the answer but suppressed it and never spoke of it with anyone.

'Why not me?' That question must have thrummed inside her throughout our holiday. With each death, she wanted to offer herself in place of the sick one. It was an old refrain: 'Take me. Take me.' Her offer was sincere, too sincere, because a part of her wanted to end her life, except pride would never allow herself to shame the family. And there were still the babies whom she loved, great-grandchildren, adult grandchildren and one baby grandchild. Melila was her new lease of life, so she spent the holiday wavering between grief for her sister and love of the children, often displaying both emotions at the same time as she held each baby and sang melancholy Yiddish songs to them. When she forgot herself, she resumed her unique chant with her soporific touch that lulled the most agitated baby, and weary parent, to sleep.

Ay li lu li lu li lu lu;
Ay li lu li lu lu …

16

IT WAS March by the time I got an appointment to the mind–body gastroenterologist, three months after my initial CT scan. I was desperately hoping for a diagnosis, so when I was informed on a phone consultation that my pain sounded like IBS, I was pleased to hear a doctor offer something more precise than laxatives.

'My cousin has Inflammatory Bowel Syndrome,' I said, pleased that the pieces were falling into place.

The correction was emphatic. 'No! IBS means Irritable Bowel Syndrome. It's very specific.'

The specificity reminded me of the village argument at the start of *Fiddler on the Roof*. Horse. Mule. Irritable. Inflammatory.

The doctor was fully booked out but told me, again by phone, that I was to have an ultrasound on my small intestine. I learned from the internet that 'small' meant long, a serpentine cord that if stretched out would cover seven metres in length. It was the cupboard for many vital organs—the liver, pancreas, bile duct—the seat of digestion. On the day of the appointment, I received a call that the doctor couldn't do it in person because a family member had COVID. A different gastroenterologist would conduct the ultrasound in their place.

The offices were pristine, clean and modern. I never learned the name of the stand-in gastroenterologist, but she talked me through the images on the screen. The good news, she began, was that the walls of my intestines hadn't thickened, indicating that I was safe from Crohn's disease. This came as a guilty relief because Gabe has Crohn's disease. I knew how debilitating it could be but his had been manageable since his diagnosis.

Pushing the ultrasound probe deep into my abdomen, she continued. To the left of the small bowel there was a clump—the usual stuff. Faecal loading. Shit.

'To the left are air bubbles. This seems to indicate a classic case of a condition called SIBO.'

'Huh?'

'Small Intestinal Bacterial Overgrowth.'

Another inquisitive grunt.

'Most of your bacteria is supposed to grow in the large intestine. When it leaks into the small one, and multiplies, then it forms gaseous pockets that can cause the kind of bloating you're experiencing.'

I felt like cheering. At last, someone with a diagnosis other than shit. This sounded scientific. She wiped down the gunk and sent me home. I immediately consulted Google. It convinced me. Even though the syndrome was usually identified through a special breath test, I trusted the intuition of the nameless gastroenterologist who had seen the pockets of gas alongside the faecal loading on the ultrasound.

The bad part of the news was that it was a syndrome that couldn't be quickly cured with a tablet. A syndrome has no cure. It can be managed. Perusing the internet, I was bombarded by a thousand modes of management, coupled with stories of people whose lives and relationships were ruined by the condition.

I thought of Michelle and me. Nothing could touch us.

In conversation with others, I learned that many people had struggled with IBS and reduced the symptoms. Someone recommended another tool: hypnotherapy. This online course offered a six-week digital series and ongoing training that research proved was more effective than drugs. The presiding gastroenterologist had already put me on one drug but the promise of a more rapid, permanent break from the pain was too enticing. I immediately downloaded the app. A soothing voice explained that this was not the kind of hypnosis one thinks of in relation to entertainment shows. The aim was to create new mind associations that would repair the channel of messages that were misleading the gut. The problem was that my pain was real and not real. It was real in that I felt it, but not real in that it was produced by nerve fibres being mixed up and sending entangled signals.

I lay on my bed and immediately started the podcast, promising that I would keep up with the recommended twenty minutes each day. A problem became immediately apparent. My back was aching too much to concentrate on the voice. I needed a solution. I was never one for baths but there was one in the bathroom which we used for Melila, waiting for her dadda. I filled it up, added crystal bath salts and placed my iPhone on the ledge. I borrowed a small loudspeaker from Melila's bedroom and paired the devices. My first thought: why had I resisted baths? It was blissful. I floated in the water, suspended in a position where the pain couldn't reach me.

The method began with ten minutes of relaxation. I was tetchy but did my best to let myself fall into relaxation. Next was a scenario into which I had to project myself as a character in a dream. In these immersive dreams the scenes were drawn out in detail. In one, I was in an old-fashioned pharmacy filled with drawers and tables cluttered with bottles of potions, vials and test tubes. My eyes were drawn to one drawer that was labelled with my name. In it was a vial just for me.

Just for me, the voice repeated softly. I felt the scene was conjured from *Aladdin*.

I drank the imaginary potion which flowed easily through my digestive tract. There was nothing impeding it. No pain. Just a flowing curative fount. Just for me.

This was followed by wake-up time. A long, drawn-out count to five, after which I could open my eyes.

The bathwater was cold by the time I stepped out. I felt refreshed and made sure that the scenario stayed in my mind for the rest of the day. Looking back, it's hard to believe that only seven months had passed since one life-changing event—the birth of Melila and my journey with Michelle into parenthood—and this new unrelenting pain.

I went back to bed. My abdomen and back were still aching. I couldn't bear the pain. Don't worry, I said. Half the trick is the diagnosis. The SIBO will be cured. I drew another hot bath and floated in it to the mellow sounds of Bach's *Cello Suites*, soothing in a situation where the doctor's suites were closed to me, as in a dream.

In my next telephone conversation with the doctor, I was told I should begin with a drug which would help my peristalsis digest the food. Soon after I would add an antibiotic used to treat SIBO but the doctor thought it best to wait so the efficacy of each drug could be independently differentiated.

A day later the pain compelled me to ring again. The receptionist told me that the doctor was busy in surgery, and that I would be contacted by the end of the day. I received a phone call after work hours, the sound of children in the background, to be told that considering my pain, it would be best not to wait and to begin both drugs at the same time. I felt relieved not having to wait when I read that the antibiotic was the best hope for speedier relief from my symptoms.

I called again a day later. I felt apologetic for nagging. The best form of communication was by email or a message to the receptionist. I still hadn't put a face to the name of the gastroenterologist who was treating me only in phone consultations, but of all the specialists I had seen this one was the first one to indirectly diagnose my condition. In my email I began by thanking the doctor. 'I've been reading about Sibo and it certainly matches my symptoms; I'm surprised no other doctor diagnosed it as you did.'

What I wrote in two successive emails is chilling to read in hindsight:

> I took half a tablet yesterday evening and was in excruciating pain for most of the night without any bowel movement … When I eat a piece of dry toast, as I did for lunch, I get painful swelling and back pain …

The continuation of the email:

> Sorry to bother you … At night I was in excruciating pain and it has persisted today. The pain is in my abdomen, and through my sternum and chest, around my ribs and back. It's unrelenting, made worse soon after I eat something.
>
> I'm hoping the medication/s will kick in, but it's the worst pain I've experienced and there's little relief.

Later that afternoon, I received an email response from the receptionist with a note from the doctor prescribing two drugs. Scripts were sent to my pharmacy. I looked up the medication and was surprised to read that the first drug also went by a name that rang a bell. Motilium. I read more about it. In addition to its properties treating nerve pain, it also stimulates the production of milk for breastfeeding mothers. It was the same drug Michelle had used for the days after the birth of Melila to see if it was possible she might produce a drop of milk. I joked with Michelle that it might not be too late for me to breastfeed Melila.

The other drug was something to ease stomach cramps. Neither helped, so the next day a new drug was introduced. While filling the script at the pharmacy I read about it. It was in the tricyclic family of drugs and used mainly as an antidepressant. I read on; it had properties that after long-term usage could ease nerve pain.

Long term.

My only recourse was to fill the bath repeatedly through the night and meditate, first to the hypnotherapy sequence, then to Johann Sebastian Bach.

17

MEANWHILE, GOOD news reached us that my son and his wife had given birth in Sydney to a girl. It was my third grandchild in five months; another playmate for Melila. They named her Ellidy Kerryn.

For a long time, we had planned to hire a house in Sydney for a month and stay with my adult kids and mother when the baby was born. But we decided it would be too much for a stampede of us to come while the freshly minted parents were settling in with a newborn. I would fly, instead, alone, but my mother insisted she wasn't going to miss out on the arrival of the first child to her first grandson on my side. Michelle oscillated between wanting to come with Melila to help look after my mother and urging me to stay in Melbourne to check into hospital because of the increased severity of my pain. We decided that she and Melila should stay at home, thinking it best for everyone. So, it was just the pair of us for a few days only. I would somehow manage to hide the pain from my mother.

Instead of hiding the ache, I vented my frustration on my mother. We stayed in a hotel in Bondi. We were given rooms on different floors, each of which required its own key card. I gave her one of mine and took one of hers so we could access one another. Despite my mother's protestations that she was autonomous, she couldn't put on her hearing aids. And they wouldn't have helped anyway because just before she left, the hearing aid on her more functioning ear stopped working and we had to send it away to be fixed. The timing couldn't have been worse for a perfect storm, which also matched the state of the weather, with the entire city flooded by an unrelenting downpour. I tried calling her room, but there was no answer.

I went down to her room at midday. She was fast asleep. I called out her name but still she didn't answer. I figured it would take over an hour after she woke for her to get ready. I still hadn't seen my new grandchild who had come home from hospital that morning. Gabi's parents had already been there to welcome the baby. I decided I'd sneak in a quick visit and then return to collect my mother.

I found her dressed and seated on the couch upon my return. She was angry and gave me an earful, 'How can you leave your mother here waiting!'

There was no use answering back, though I'm sure I muttered something that in her deafness she managed to decipher. I tried to lift her spirits by signalling that the baby was at home waiting to see her.

'How can I go without eating?' she said. 'Do you want to starve me?'

'I'll stop on the way and get you coffee and a sandwich.'

Needless to say, she didn't like the coffee or the sandwich.

But the baby was anything but phuy, her Yiddish word for something one spits out. She swallowed it up with love, kissed it repeatedly, examined it and approved of its beauty. There was still one more grand gesture to perform, the reason she had come all the way to Sydney. The reason, she said dramatically, she had stayed alive till this day.

The parents filled a small bathtub and propped it next to the kitchen sink. They immersed Ellidy as though she was being baptised and my mother did what she had done to every baby in our line of Polish succession. She scrubbed the baby's brains with shampoo into its keppeleh—its head, so that she would not only be beautiful but would also join the pantheon of geniuses in our family. If my mother lived long enough, Ellidy would no doubt be ranked among the other great-grandchildren and one baby grandchild by her cleverness, which began by comparing subtle developments that hinted at their future academic achievements in school and later university.

Finally, we went back to the hotel.

'I'm starving,' she said, 'and I want to look at that other hotel we stay at. I'm sure it's nicer. We can walk there.'

'It was booked out, Mum. I tried.'

'So we can walk there.'

'It's pouring.'

'Never mind. We have to eat anyway.'

We must have been the only people walking in the wind and rain. My mother is persistent.

While I ordered her takeaway from a Chinese restaurant, she slipped into the hotel lobby. She emerged with her predetermined verdict.

'Much nicer. Where we're staying is a hole by comparison.'

'Ours is actually more expensive,' I said.

'A waste of money,' she shrugged.

When we returned to the hotel, we walked several feet apart along the narrow hallway, where I accompanied her to her room.

'Tomorrow pick me up on time.'

'What time is that?' I asked.

'When I'm awake.'

The following day I emailed the gastroenterologist:

> I'm in Sydney for my son's newborn, back on the weekend. I've been in debilitating pain much of the time and want your advice on things I can do … to exclude anything sinister? I desperately need to get on top of this as it's impossible to function normally.

What stands out in my email is the use of the word 'sinister'. I had tried to avoid complaining about the possibility that something other than IBS was causing the pain. But from the outset, when I went for the initial CT scan, consulted the doctor who gave me the colonoscopy, made appointments with three GPs, and now put my health in the hands of a gastroenterologist who remained faceless, I had harboured the fear that I might have cancer. I was a 62-year-old father living the life of a 42-year-old. My father had died at ninety-two. My mother, despite her threats that life wasn't worth living, was eighty-seven. That was my future. I felt like a hypochondriac complaining.

The answer to my email came at the end of the workday in a terse response from the receptionist, which surely counts as Exhibit Nine: An order to increase the prescribed antidepressants.

I instinctively felt reluctant to triple my dosage without direct discussion. Instead, I doubled it as a compromise. The question that haunts me is why I submitted to this particular doctor, and even more to the medical fraternity as a whole, when my symptoms were so severe?

The next day I made sure I picked up my mother by midday, assuming I would have to wake her.

She was sitting on the couch. 'From 10 a.m.,' she yelled, tapping her watch. She was hungry. It was a repeat of the previous day.

So too was my night a repeat, only worse. I realised I had run out of pain relief. It must have been two in the morning, freezing, when I went outside in search of a pharmacy. No luck.

The following morning, I wrote what the receptionist must have regarded as a tiresome email. I even acknowledged that I was becoming a nagger with my daily email.

> Last night was the worst it's been. I was up till 4am—writhing in pain—had 3 baths and 2 showers as that helps a bit. Woke from pain again after 2 hours sleep.
>
> I'm back in Melbourne tomorrow but I'm not functioning at all. If it remains bad on the weekend, should I go to hospital for pain relief? I'm writing this because I've never experienced anything like it—it feels like my inside kishkes [intestines] are going to explode from my stomach and back spasms.
>
> Again, sorry to nag but I'm not tolerating the pain (and it reminds me too much of what I've seen in recent years). I know Sibo can be debilitating but the intensity worries me.

This time, I hinted at the sinister thing I feared in brackets. The farfetched possibility of a third in a row. Why was I afraid to say the word? Death.

After five days, it was time to go home. I was in love with my granddaughter, but my relationship with my mother, who had always appreciated the care I gave her, was stretched to the limit. She ignored me in the car on the way to the airport, on the plane, on the drive to her home, and when I carried her luggage to her apartment. I returned home into the arms of my loved ones but they could no longer soothe my pain. I was more desperate for a bath than to see my own baby daughter and wife.

Michelle was obviously very worried. She pressed on me to call the doctor and demand a face-to-face consultation. If I didn't do it, she added, then she would. Her determination made resistance futile. It was early April and a couple more tests were arranged, this time using a pillcam, an inventive miniature camera that takes pictures of the small bowel. The pill was kept in a case like Cinderella's slipper. After swallowing it, I carried an electronic device around with me till the end of the day. I waited anxiously for the results, hoping that it might identify something—even that sinister thing. The results came in an email from the doctor forwarded by the receptionist: 'The pillcam was normal. No more antibiotics. I will contact him later.'

When was later? Still, I persisted with the one last test that the gastroenterologist booked. An MRI to check if the source of the pain was a slipped disc that was radiating to my stomach. I managed to get the only available booking for a scan. It was a 9.30 time slot—p.m., that is. The pain was so bad that I paced the waiting room like a feral animal. It reached unbearable proportions while I was in the MRI tunnel and I struggled to respond to the

Wizard of Oz voice that boomed its command. 'Breathe. Now hold your breath. Breathe.'

The email response to my desperate request for the outcome showed that my back was fine.

Exhibit Number Ten: 'Please note we endeavour to respond to all email enquiries within 48 hours. If your matter is urgent, please call us directly.'

18

THE FOLLOWING week was a chaotic clash of holidays when institutions were short-staffed. Easter clashed with Passover which clashed with Anzac Day. There was one more person I hadn't called and who could squeeze me in before the onset of the holidays. My childhood friend, Henry, a distinguished gastroenterologist. I had decided long ago that I didn't want friends looking up my butthole. His success, my mother liked to say, could be attributed to the fact that he was the only baby outside our family whose brains she had scrubbed with shampoo. As kids, we used to go on family holidays together. We would laugh at our parents' accents as they struggled to navigate the new countries we visited. Some of my best memories are holidays with Henry. I was about to embark on a different kind of journey with him, urged by my family and friends.

I called his office and his secretary answered. It happened to be his wife, who worked part-time there while doubling as a speech therapist. She too was a dear and close friend, a romantic flame from my teen years. I quickly explained that I desperately needed to see him. An appointment was made for the next morning.

I relayed the story to Henry, and watched as he raised his eyebrows. And then he said what no other doctor had said. 'It doesn't make sense. We're starting over with an MRI. I want to see all the tests that you've done. And we're going to do your bloods again.'

I breathed a sigh of relief, but also trepidation.

'We'll start off with an MRI. It's hard to get in but don't worry, I'll arrange it for you next week on Easter Tuesday when a semblance of routine returns.'

I counted the days on my fingers under his desk. Six. I feared what games my abdomen and back would play in those waiting days. My one distraction was our plans for a Passover Seder dinner—which this year, according to the lunar calendar, fell on Good Friday—with family at our home.

Two years earlier, Michelle had tried to cement our blended families by inviting sixty people. We erected a tent on our rooftop, decorated it Moroccan style, and invited every branch of our family—Johnny's, Kerryn's, my mother's Krochmal side, Michelle's family. It was a superhuman feat on Michelle's part, a gesture that proclaimed we were one family. Our voices could be heard singing contemporary Jewish and Israeli melodies across the rooftop accompanied by the roar of the screamers on the Luna Park trains. For that night, we could imagine that none of the linked carriages in our clan had unfastened.

Due to my pain this year, we moved the Seder from our home to Yael's home at the last moment. My

Melbourne-based elder kids came, a welcome sign that they were integrating into a new branch of the family. We knew the twin babies wouldn't last long. But it was I who left early because of my pain, walking Melila home and putting her to bed by myself. If it had been possible, I would have let my baby put me to bed.

As the chant recited by the youngest child goes, 'Mah Nishtana halayla hazeh?' 'Why is this night different from all other nights?'

While waiting for the post-holiday MRI organised by Henry, I had one more appointment that I'd booked a month before. Michelle and others had been pushing me to see a general physician: someone whose eyes were trained to sift through all the information and dissect it from scratch. For his status, I was surprised by the shabbiness of his city office. I didn't have to fill in my history; he had treated everyone in my family, especially my mother. I told him about the pain.

The Pain.

A manila folder filled with my documents was strategically placed on his desk. He fired a few medical questions at me and then gave me his diagnosis.

Exhibit Number Eleven: 'You've gone through a lot these past few years,' he began, tapping on the folder. 'Endless trauma. I can understand why you fear that you might have cancer. But I've looked at the scans since December and they show nothing. If you had a tumour in your body, they'd show like rat's balls. But there's nothing. I'm not saying you don't feel the pain, but it's psychosomatic. And perfectly understandable in the light of your experience.'

I didn't tell him that Henry had already ordered a battery of tests to check if my psychosomatic symptoms might be ruled out by proper medical analysis.

I walked forlornly through the dank corridors of this esteemed physician. His folder made me think of a wealthy benefactor whose shelves in his grandiose mansion were filled with decorative book covers, concealing blank pages. In any case, whatever the doctor might have discovered in his file, it was too damn late.

One hundred and twenty-two days had passed since my original CT scan. One hundred and twenty-two days and not a single doctor responded to my request for an MRI scan on my organs in all that time, through all my unbearable pain.

Until now.

MRI Day came around three days later. It was Friday 22 April, a day before Melila turned eight months. Half of her life was spent with her father in debilitating pain.

By the afternoon of the scan, Henry's secretary called. It wasn't his wife this time but a stranger's voice. She spoke in a warm but professional manner.

'Dr Debinski would like you to come in to discuss your results.' And then words that I knew spelled my fate. 'And he's asked if you can bring your wife with you.'

'Let's not jump to conclusions,' Michelle comforted me, but I could see in her eyes that she was the one who might require comfort. We waited out the few hours and arrived at his office. From the corner of my eye, I could see Henry fidgeting at his desk. Within minutes we were whisked in.

I knew how to read Henry. The back of his neck was red. He was nervous but spoke in a calm voice learned from experience. But what kind of experience does it take to break the news he harboured to a friend?

It took him some time to get to the crux of the matter. 'We've looked at all the scans. Three doctors have studied it from December and the CT from then is pristine clear. Nothing. But the MRI shows', he paused, 'that you have a tumour. It's five centimetres long. On your pancreas. The good news is that it hasn't metastasised. It's sitting at the centre, which explains why you're not jaundiced.'

Five centimetres!

Another vocabulary rushed to me from the past: what the fuck?

I didn't say it out loud. The best word for my reaction was one of bewilderment. Something was seriously wrong. We'd talked about pancreatitis but that was different from pancreatic cancer. I was numb. It didn't feel possible, but I immediately pictured my death. The only question in my mind was if I would last as long as Kerryn and Johnny.

In the background, Henry's voice: 'We can't be sure yet until we conduct an endoscopic biopsy and a PET scan.'

'But you know already. It's malignant. How did I go from having a clear CT in December to a five-centimetre tumour in April?'

'It's our working assumption. We need to book an appointment with an oncologist.' He mentioned Kerryn's and Johnny's oncologist.

'I think I need a new face,' I said. What I meant was a different outcome. Would he take me on a third cancer journey to the grave?

'Best you stay in hospital overnight,' Henry advised, 'so we can start checking you thoroughly.'

I ended up in a double room with an old priest who farted all night. It didn't bother me. I had speakers covering my ears channelling Bach and I'd already cocooned myself in an alternative world conjured by Mozart's *Requiem*.

I had made a promise to my children. No secrets. They were anxiously waiting for the results and calling incessantly. We organised a group call. Michelle directed me to the only private space available, a storage room filled with every imaginable shape of wheelchair. We had to stand among the clutter as my kids bombarded me with questions.

Slowly, I let out the news. I had a tumour. It hadn't metastasised. It might be lymphoma, which was treatable. They could all see through the evasive code.

Gabe was numb. He asked Gabi to digest the news for him. She is a trained radiation-oncologist with a special research interest in pancreatic cancer.

Sarah burst into tears: 'This is as bad as linitis plastica'—Kerryn's rare form of gastric cancer. 'Worse,' she said.

'Does this mean we're going to be orphans?' said Rachel, her sobbing audible.

'Just when things were getting good again,' Sarah lamented through her tears.

'We're all going to die within the next twenty years,' said Rachel, as though what was happening was a curse or a game of pass the parcel.

I didn't know how to comfort them. I had the words for them when Kerryn was diagnosed, but this time I was the sick one. I was too overwhelmed to do anything, except say, 'I love you all.'

The endoscopy came back confirming it was pancreatic cancer—not the more hopeful possibility of lymphoma but adenocarcinoma. Bad news—very bad news. I was treated to the one silver lining in the cloud: an upgrade to the new oncology ward, which resembled a hotel.

I kept thinking, this can't be happening. I was invulnerable. The odds of another person in one family being hit by terminal cancer seemed impossible.

A memory rose to the surface. One that I had repressed.

My father had survived Auschwitz with one family member. The rest, including his mother and younger sisters, were gassed in Treblinka. Only my father and his devout brother, Boruch, survived. They protected one another in the camps and after several years in Switzerland migrated to Australia.

What I'd repressed was that my uncle, in whose household I spent much time, had fallen ill in his mid-fifties. I recall seeing my indefatigable aunty holding him by the arm and doing slow circle laps in their living room. He looked like one of the walking dead from the camps, what they called a Musselman.

No one told him the cause of his illness. They wanted to protect him.

I remember, too, the night of the phone call that came four months later. I woke my father who wept for the one surviving remnant of his family whose luck and life prematurely ended.

Only after he died was his illness named. Pancreatic cancer.

Breathe. Now hold your breath. Breathe deeply.

Had I fallen victim to the Baker gene, the obvious but unthinkable reality? My father was the lucky one who defied the odds. No wonder he died playing on a pokie machine.

That first night of the rest of my life I sobbed in my hospital bed. I yearned for a diagnosis of rat's arses. The child in me cried to my Daddy but it was too late for him to answer me.

REVELATION

19

MY BODY is quivering uncontrollably from rigours. Someone drapes a warm blanket over my shoulders but it doesn't quell the shivers. Nurses in chequered shirts, like a bloodied chessboard, surround me. An orderly helps me onto a wheelchair and guides me out of my room. I'm in a daze. The route is familiar but the pictures on the wall are hazy. When was I last here? It was this morning.

The verdict rings in my ears over and over. Pancreas. Pancreas. Pancreas. In the holy tongue, my luvluv.

My teeth are chattering as I thank the orderly. A nurse approaches. 'Your name.'

I answer.

'Date of birth.'

I can barely get the words out. I hear a voice say it for me. It is Michelle, my lovelove. She has accompanied me the whole way. The shivering continues but I feel calmer for having her there.

Eventually, a nurse takes over. I'm guided into a room that looks like an extraterrestrial compound. A machine in the middle. I lie down but the pain cuts through my abdomen and spine. I want the magician to slice me in half and sew me back together again.

Abracadabra. The source of that powerful word comes from the Hebrew phrase 'Adaber Kediber'. I will speak it and will come to be.

Adaber Kediber, I whisper to myself, luvluv no more.

A contraption slides me into a tunnel. Close the lid and I'll be gone. The pain will cease. And abracadabra, the lid opens and I'm cleansed, the chills thawed.

Michelle is waiting for me and holds my hand.

'Where's Melila?' I ask.

'At home. Don't worry.'

'Does she know?' I stupidly ask, and then add, 'My kids. My poor children.'

I am returned to my ward and a nurse cheerfully checks that all the IV tubes attached to the multi-pronged hanger are untangled. When they cinch, the machine beeps. I manoeuvre my hand to silence it but nothing helps. It joins an orchestral sound in the corridor from all the adjoining rooms, as if clamouring for a collective escapade of suffering patients.

That night a familiar face visits me, the head of palliative care who had guided Kerryn during the last ten months of her life. She had done the same for Johnny. This time, she sits on the edge of my bed and holds my hand.

'I don't want pain,' I say, repeating the same words Kerryn had used seven years earlier.

'You know we'll look after you,' she answers.

I understand what she means. I recall how precise she was in prognosticating the time Kerryn had left when I asked if she thought we could manage an overseas trip to attend my nephew's wedding.

'Mark,' she had said in a semi-private consultation room, 'have you seen her scans?'

It sounded part reprimand, part a call to realism.

Then came the promise given directly to Kerryn, who feared blockages from her condition and possible operations to relieve them. For her, that was the cut-off line, the get-me-out-of-here clause I'd somehow promised to honour for her. At the time, there was no Voluntary Assisted Dying Act in our part of the country, a euphemism for euthanasia. So I googled and found a pill that I could import from China, in case it came to it.

Talk of euthanasia is anathema to the head of palliative care. She works in a Catholic hospital founded by nuns from Italy. More than that, she is a professional pain-relief doctor who believes that palliation is possible in every circumstance.

'Every case is unique,' she assures me. 'There is a chance we can shrink the tumour because it hasn't metastasised. Hopefully, we can get you to an operable stage.'

I nod at the realisation that unlike Kerryn and Johnny, whose chances of survival were deemed nil when they were diagnosed, I am being told I still have odds. Whether they are worth betting on is another question.

I lie in bed, writhing in pain. When I'm asked to score my pain out of ten I manage to find the words: 'Twenty.'

The pain is off the scale and I'm not sure I have the energy or will to fight. I've seen the trick too many times. Palliation for a period of months until you're ready to surrender to your fate.

I'm too confused to realise that I'm stuck in the past. I'm not facing the prospect of being a widower for a second time round. I'm the one facing death. It's Michelle and Melila who will be left to grieve me, along with my adult children and mother. How will Melila survive without a father, who will forever remain an implanted memory of a childhood Dadda?

I have no choice. I have to bet on myself for her sake. Is that why a gambler calls it shaking the die?

The doctor unclasps my hand. She hasn't answered my question about my prognosis. I sense that she is lying, but understand she has no choice.

'Don't forget me,' I say. 'You're a busy person.'

'You have my word. I'll always tell you the truth.'

She leaves me alone; I can hear fluttering shadows on the ceiling, but I know it's just the shifting darkness, and my body, trembling from terror and disease.

An army of doctors files through my room.

First come the infectious disease experts. The next team is of respiratory specialists. They are convinced I have an infection that is preventing me from starting chemotherapy. The conveyance back and forth for scans feels like I'm spinning on a ride. I could be at home, watching myself from my chair at the window whirring on the carousel horse at Luna Park, a child again. I'm wheeled in and out for more tests in search of the mysterious infection.

Finally, they reach the conclusion I have organising pneumonia. I tell a doctor that I had plain disorganised pneumonia three years earlier. My symptoms were obvious then—sweats, coughing and, worst of all, wheezing and crackling from my lungs. It was the Jewish month of Rosh Hashana, the New Year, when it is the custom to blow a ram's horn producing an array of raw musical notations. I spent my nights holding my iPhone to my chest and taping the crackles that produced a simulacrum of these ancient sounds.

Why is no one asking about my pancreatic tumour?

The nurses add a liquid punching bag of strong antibiotics to my steel tripod. Butterfly cannulas are needled into both sides of my hips.

How much time has passed?

I fall into a deep sleep. When I wake, I don't know where I am. Is it day or night?

I can't even reach for the bedside remote control because I've forgotten it's there. By chance a nurse walks in, summoned by the beep on the stand. She can see I'm confused. She calls in another nurse. I say I need to go to the bathroom. They lift me out of bed but I've forgotten why I'm standing. They hold me around the shoulders and guide me out of bed. It's too late. My pyjamas—airline trackies—are dripping wet. Who is this incontinent person? Thankfully, I have the presence of mind to tell myself, 'It's not me, it's my cancer.'

For now, however, it's me, and I'm frightened as hell.

Only a day earlier—or is it weeks?—I used to give Melila nightly baths. Michelle and I marvelled at the dependency of our baby on the two of us, her parents. Now it is me who is dependent on others. I have reverted to my beginnings.

One night when I open my eyes, I find a yellow stick-it note pinned to the bathroom door by my elder daughters, Sarah and Rachel, who are concerned about my state of delirium:

I'm in hospital.
All is OKAY
If worried—call Michelle
Deep breaths
We love you

My new home is a hospital bed. Michelle cohabits my bedroom ward with me most of the time. Sometimes Melila visits. How will she cope with the dramatic change in my status? Until now, I have been an active father, taking advantage of the flexibility that my lifestyle at age sixty affords me. I never missed a single appointment to the doctor with her during Michelle's pregnancy and after her birth. I attended visits to the maternal child health clinic, fed her with a bottle and at night I took it in turns with Michelle putting Melila to sleep. I'd dance with her after baths to Beatles songs, our favourite being 'Hey Jude'. We parented equally for the most part, an experience I regret that my career pressures didn't allow thirty years ago with my adult kids. Has all this active involvement come to an end?

When we talked about our baby before she was born Michelle used to say the first two years are the most formative. Who knows if Melila will even turn two by the time I die? What I know with certainty is that the formative years we had dreamed of giving our baby have been replaced by a nightmare. Will she remember the trauma of what she cannot possibly understand as our morning walks through the spacious streets of home are replaced by the four walls of a hospital room? Can she see the figure of Jesus hanging on one of the walls?

Crash.

I think I've woken from a dream, but the Jesus crucifix has mysteriously fallen from the nail on which it hangs and smashed onto the ground. I'm convinced it must be an omen, but of what I cannot say. I can't get out of bed to return it to its respectful place. When I wake the crucifix is gone. Someone has swept it from the floor and removed it from the room. I want it overlooking me, but I'm ashamed to admit that I'm groping for a miracle from another religion. It's all I've got. After all, the sages of my own religion long ago concluded that there are no miracles in our days.

Finally, after three weeks in hospital, I am deemed ready for chemotherapy. To feed the chemicals through me, my body is drilled and fastened with trinkets: a blue and red lumen dangling like a bracelet from my right arm, and two bright yellow butterfly cannulas, one on each hip. If I did the hula I'm sure I'd be able to gather all the nurses and doctors into a long conga line.

I am to be given the standard assault for pancreatic cancer with a regime called Folforinox. It is made up of five different components. Everything in medicine is coded in acronyms and unpronounceable words that usually contain the letter X—a winner in a Scrabble game. I'm in too much pain to have the chemotherapy administered from a chair. I lie on a hospital bed, Michelle seated by my side for the five-plus hours it takes to administer the chemo drugs. She helps me in every way possible with food supplies, which we laugh about because at home I would never eat in bed and allow it to be messed up with crumbs. Despite the well-equipped hospital room, I should confess that I brought with me my own pillows and matching doona. All the more reason why I will not allow a morsel of food to sully my sheets. The fluids press heavily on my bladder so several times I have to unplug myself and manoeuvre my steel mannequin with its swollen plastic bags to the bathroom. The urge is so intense there is some leakage once again. Not just leakage, cytotoxic leakage. So much for my clean sheets.

But what I fear most is touching my baby—contaminating Melila with poisonous, healing fluids. I am a danger to my daughter who only one month ago, I smothered in a million kisses.

It comes back in fragments through the fog of chemotherapy and morphine, the fight I put up to control the medications that manage my pain. At first the doctors try Fentanyl patches which supply a constant flow of relief that is invisible to me. The pain breaks through and my body arches from the agony. I want to press a physical button, to adjust the pain levels as required so that the relief is tangible. I bargain like I'm in a Turkish bazaar and we settle on a higher dose of subcutaneous breakthrough injections. I am also given a driver. Not a chauffeur to take me around Melbourne but a rectangular perspex container that connects directly to my left butterfly.

20

THE NAUSEA I feared from chemotherapy never comes; it is the one symptom that doesn't strike me. Instead, the side effects choose another end of my body from which to exit copiously. Chemo, for me and countless others, produces an 'excremental assault' on your body, an expression coined by Terence Des Pres in his classic book, *The Survivor*. I must have shat out enough to flood the Yarra River. At one point, I am waking every two hours to fill the toilet bowl. The one thing I share with Melila are soft wet wipes with small teddy bear imprints. I rip through a box a day with an added application of barrier cream.

I have to rank the excrement according to the Bristol Stool Chart, which I presume most Bristolians don't realise is a claim to fame for their city. Number one is for constipated formed stool; seven is for the liquified type, with every formation in between. A schoolteacher would be pleased that I consistently scored the highest number. I am also supposed to record the volume on a chart. Short of scooping out the muddy river of stool from the toilet bowl, a feat I witnessed a heroic nurse perform, raising my estimation of nurses higher than any doctor, I have to guess the volume. I simply write one of four measurements in increments of a quarter, but I get sick of looking at my undigested produce, so I guesstimate the amount based on the time my evacuations last.

This is accompanied by convulsive sounds that seem to detonate from every orifice. An involuntary burp can outdo the rapturous finale of the Seven Tenors, or in my case, the Seven Baritones. Of the other exit point for gas, I won't go into details. They are not me. They are my cancer.

Tiredness. I wish I could capture the extremities of that word's meaning. One minute you have energy, the next it slips out of you and you can barely walk. My eyes close on me. I often fall asleep with a computer on my lap. The feeling of depletion can also be exacerbated by the top-up hydromorphone that Michelle injects subcutaneously. We both know that once I take one, it's straight to bed. To get ahead, I am usually injected in bed to save me the effort of moving.

Over time, I get other side effects. I feel like I am wearing socks on my feet and that I'm walking in gravelly sand. I wonder if the cure is to walk barefoot in actual sand on the principle of a double negative equals a positive. This is all the start of peripheral neuropathy which kills my nerve endings, temporarily or permanently. My toes feel like bunched up cauliflower. Every night, Michelle rubs cream into my hands and feet, or cuts my nails, like a baby. It is the most loving gesture. She observes that Melila and I have the same toenails and fingernails. Melila learns to massage me.

Then there is the loss of hair. The first to go, to my astonishment, is my nasal hair. I only notice it because my nose drips incessantly and I'm constantly dabbing at it with a tissue. So much to learn—the obscure purpose of our internal features, the order of things. This is followed by strangely shaped patches of hair disappearing from my legs, my upper body, and then my genitals. The hair on my head gradually thins. Then I lose it altogether. In my family my hair is my distinguishing feature, though it has lost its trademark colour; in my fifties it changed from grey to silvery white. I am beginning to look more like my brother. His revenge from the grave. Finally, I shave it all off.

I wept when knowledge of my diagnosis first began to sink in, but now most of the time my lachrymal glands are blocked. One night Dahlia came to the hospital and we embraced. Tears flowed. I looked for mine after she had gone and squeezed out the gland. For the next year, I rarely cry.

The proclamation of my disease at first stays within narrow circles. Slowly, word spreads until the gossip mill is running at full speed. Messages pour in. Some sound like farewell notes, as in bye-bye forever, you've been a great influence on me.

People are bewildered. How could this be happening to one family? I share their astonishment but don't answer any of the messages. I'm exhausted, still in pain and I have a pretext, like a mother's school note for my antisocial behaviour. In fact, what I desperately need is an absentee note to excuse me from my mother, who has checked herself into a room in the same hospital as a way of being close to me. At least, that is how I interpret her sudden need for emergency care in an adjacent ward.

Since returning from Sydney, we have made up.

Making up with my mother means lots of slobbery kisses and declarations of love for me, which I in turn must reciprocate. But I don't have the strength—or is it will?—to drag myself out of my hospital bed and make the neighbourly visit to her ward. Finally, with Michelle's help, I manage the journey. I leave my wheelchair outside her room. Michelle holds me so I can maintain the pantomime of wellness but I can't hide the wires attached to my body.

My mother kisses my hand repeatedly like I'm royalty. 'You have to promise me you'll get well. You have so much to live for.'

'I'm doing my best,' I answer.

'I can't live without you. If something happens to you I'll kill myself.'

'Mum, don't talk that way. You're strong. Very strong.'

'Without you, I have nothing. Tell me the truth, what does Henry say?'

I am forced into a white lie. 'The doctor says the therapy will help.'

I can't even bring myself to say chemotherapy, in order to maintain the deception. How can I tell her at this stage that she might be forced to bury not one but two sons?

Exhausted by the cancer and her understandable emotions, I wrench my hand away to go back to my room. As I leave, I hear her repeating the story about how she had washed Henry's hair as a baby, so for sure he will be able to fix me.

She stays in hospital for a week, during which I only visit her twice because I am too weak to move. Or is it that I am too weak to face her and acknowledge the guilt I feel for the affliction I am causing her and others? We get her consent to move her into temporary respite in an aged-care home. She hates it, she tells her grandchildren, gritting her teeth, but for the first time in ages I am told she is acting socially. One of the first people she'd befriended when she came to Australia, Bluma, has been there for some time and shows her the ropes.

After a meal declared inedible by the two of them, my mother and Bluma with her pushcart raid the kitchen late at night like two school-campers and fill the trolley basket with sandwiches. A visit from a grandchild finds her attending a concert of Hebrew songs. They have to drag my mother out. While she scoffs at the concert, she still can't resist boasting that she is the only one who knows the words to the songs. My mother also starts to dress up and use her dentures, a deliberate exhibition to demonstrate that she is above the people around her, whom she regards as rotting to death. She keeps on repeating that from here there is only one place left to go: the cemetery.

She insists that she be given another chance in her home before deciding whether to move permanently to the aged-care home. It doesn't help when a single COVID case forces all the residents to remain alone in their rooms for three days. Gone are the midnight fridge raids and concerts.

'This place is like a prison,' she says from her bed on FaceTime. She has let herself go again. Her hair is wild and she doesn't bother with her dentures. I empathise fully with her situation. The problem is that she doesn't have all the facts before her. In her mind, I am going to be cured. We all collude in avoiding mention of the offending word—pancreas.

But she knows, because nothing ever passes her eyes.

I luvluv my mother.

I let her brush her lips against the back of my legs, like a baby.

I am regressing. Soon I will out-baby my baby.

Halfway through one of my chemotherapy infusions, my oncologist's registrar visits. He has a difficult gig; he happens to know my kids socially and is familiar with me. At our first meeting he asks if I feel comfortable working with him. I don't hesitate. I can see immediately he is the sweetest and most caring doctor. He proves to be more than that because he hasn't yet learned to pull up the drawbridge of emotion. He is still innocent, and has a baby at home the same age as Melila. It will only be a matter of time until he will have to learn the art of self-protection; or maybe his character will always connect deeply with others, and make him emotionally available for support.

He stops by for a short visit during my five-hour treatment, medical folder and iPad in his arms. He passes on some important information about my blood cells going up. Or is it down? It doesn't matter because Michelle writes everything on her phone and then posts it to our family, an act of love and mercy in the guise of detached competence.

I take advantage of a pause in the conversation and ask the hard questions. I have two questions for him. The first, which I want to get off my chest, is whether an earlier diagnosis might have made a difference. By difference, I mean between life and death. I know it's a question he won't or can't answer. He hints, emms and ahhs, and says something about my intelligence being able to answer that myself. I nod, and as a fellow Jew, I quote from the Talmud: hamevin yavin—the one who understands, understands. And I understand enough. When I tell people the story of my misdiagnosis, they are furious and urge me to sue for malpractice. But I refuse to face the challenges ahead of me filled with bile. Ironically, I need instead to worry about the workings of my own bile which could easily malfunction, setting off a chain reaction of complications.

The second question is harder. I asked him to tell me honestly what the prognosis is. Michelle's eyes dart my way. 'You shouldn't think about this stuff during chemo. Let it do its work.'

The first thing the registrar asks is if Michelle is up to hearing it. She nods. 'I want to hear what Mark hears.'

Then he does something which shows a maturity beyond his experience. Like a character in a movie, he unmasks himself. He knows that if he is going to speak honestly with me, I have to see his eyes and face, COVID regulations aside.

I don't learn anything I don't already know. Hamevin yavin, but I need to hear it. No person is only a statistic. There are always outliers. My chances of operability are five per cent. One in twenty. I am ready to race for those odds. He reiterates it will take more than even radical shrinkage of the tumour to make that possible.

I understand.

But the hardest part of his answer for me is that the tumour would have to do somersaults and unwrench itself from my arteries. Fifty per cent of people with pancreatic cancer live up to a year, he continues.

'Six to nine months on average,' I correct him, based on my extensive internet research.

I can see his eyes water. I feel guilty for not crying when he is talking about me. He returns his mask to his face. He is once more a faceless doctor, but I know what lies behind the mask, and deeper inside his heart.

'I need to go to the bathroom,' I say to Michelle. 'This fluid is pressing hard on me. Can you help me get up?'

She holds me with one arm, and slides the tripod stand with the other and guides me to the bathroom. When I come out of the toilet she turns on the tap water to measure the temperature in case it is too cold for my hands to withstand, an adverse effect of one of the chemotherapy drugs.

I had long ago realised that the dimensions of Michelle's heart can never be measured. Despite everything, I feel blessed.

21

AFTER NEARLY a month in hospital, I am discharged. Finally, I can kiss Melila and play with her in our own environment. I barely walk through the door of my home and I have to race to the bathroom. I sit on the seat like Rodin's thinker, wanting to cry for the way my bodily needs dominate everything.

I am still extremely frail. Palliative nurses come and visit every two days to change the drugs in my driver and top up supplies of syringes and needles for the hydromorphone that Michelle injects for breakthrough pain. The nurses all recognise me, having treated Kerryn or Johnny or both. One even remembers which room Johnny occupied during a brief stay at the palliative hospice.

We order cartons and cartons of French protein drinks to make sure I am getting enough nutrition after losing nine kilograms. The kitchen is lined with tubs and containers for all the medication, fighting for room on the benchtop alongside the bottles, teats and sterilising machine. Michelle has put up whiteboards on which to write charts that monitor my symptoms and alleviations: top-up medications for pain, my diarrhoea, my weight, my mouth ulcers, my blood pressure, my food intake, my everything. The days are consumed by check-ups, long sleeps and time with Melila, either reading to her or watching her eat in her highchair.

Michelle devotes herself to caring for me and Melila. She cancels teaching and research commitments indefinitely. Luckily, we are surrounded by family who step in to help. But the burden on them is high and unrelenting. We therefore decide to employ a nanny. Her name is Anusha and she was in her early twenties. She was born in Nepal but spent most of her life in Finland. Within days she an Melila had fallen in love, Anusha only a fraction more quickly.

Melila doesn't go to indoor play activities or socialise with other babies except for her niece and nephews because we are worried about her bringing illness into the home, especially over the winter months. Dahlia requires an operation for breast cancer and one on her leg. Rai's subtle shakes have grown more pronounced and he is sometimes unsteady on his feet. The neurologists finally determine that he has Parkinson's disease. And Yael, who dedicates herself to care of her husband, daughters and grandchildren, is also desperately in need of rest. One can see the strain of all the illnesses on her face, the strain of silence, the selfless mother whose love has no boundaries.

I encourage my children to continue living normal lives and to work hard in their careers, but they often can't see past their tears. Gabe, Gabi and Ellidy had moved to Melbourne upon my diagnosis, an ominous sign. As for my mother, she is planning to escape from her Alcatraz, the luxurious wing of the aged-care home. Despite the fact that everyone has avoided discussing the seriousness of my illness in her presence, she knows. She moves between uncontrolled grief at the prospect of losing her baby son and the hope that he will achieve a miracle and get well.

'You are my lifeline. You have so much to live for. You have a beautiful life and so much to offer.' That becomes her constant refrain: it expresses at one and the same time the determination that her words should make reality as she wishes it to be, and the lament that she knows in her heart that they can't.

I do my best with my waning energy. I read Melila my favourite books and tell her that Gaga, her name for her elder brother, Gabe, and Sezzy and Rachi, used to read the same books. I lie on the floor with her, or she sits on my lap, and we read *The Very Hungry Caterpillar*. Dadda's favourite book is *Caps for Sale*, about the peddler who balances dozens of caps on his head that are snitched by monkeys in a tree. I take out my collection of cancer caps I have bought to cover my baldness and pile them on my head so that Melila can play the role of the monkeys and tsz, tsz, knock them off my head.

While Michelle was pregnant we had travelled to Sydney, where I bought Melila an early edition of one of the *Secret Seven* books. It was ragged and the picture on the cover was exactly as I remembered it, drawn in a cartoonish way. I longed to read it to her one day, and inscribed the book on the inside cover to our unborn child: 'I wish I could give you this present while you're curled comfortably in Mummy's womb, so instead I'll read it to you through her tummy,' I wrote, adding how these books had planted in me a lifetime passion for reading and eventually writing.

I want everything that I had as a child for Melila: the albums I played in my bedroom on a small, mottled grey record-player—*Mary Poppins*, Jerry Lewis and, later, *Cabaret*—family holidays to Queensland and a memorable safari in Kenya with her elder siblings, where the animals in the books we read came to life in their natural surrounds. I dream about taking these same holidays with Melila and my grandchildren, whose names she has learned to pronounce over time: Alva, Miro and Ellidy. All this I dream for Melila, but most often I dream that she will grow up with the guidance and love of two parents, and that one day she will be led down the wedding aisle by her mother and father, her MammaDadda.

Reality refuses to let me dream. A fever covers me in sweat before my second round of chemotherapy. I am rushed to the emergency department and spend another week in hospital. Is this going to be the rhythm of my new life? Two days of fatigue, decline, infection, a week of hospitalisation, two days home. Chemo again. An immediate vision of Melila with only Mamma by her side.

I am once again locked in a compact room with a view of the distant hill, teasing me with the promise of life, something that feels unattainable despite all the pep talks that I can knock this tumour out of the ring. Michelle spends most of the time by my side, driving home reluctantly to give Yael and Dahlia a break from babysitting. The angel gene runs in the family.

For my next round of chemotherapy, the oncologist reduces the assault of toxicity by twenty per cent. 'There's no use having you come to hospital each time dehydrated and with an infection,' I'm told.

I try to do the maths in my head to calculate how that might affect my already doomsday prospects of making it to an operation. It doesn't matter, I say to myself. I am in for the fight, though I don't believe positive thinking can be transmitted to a random mutated cell. Kerryn and Johnny had given it everything and, in the end, the cancer did what it does.

Part of giving it all is exploring other options. People send me the names of top surgeons who have operated successfully on people with the same condition as me. We decide to consult one such surgeon so we can be on his radar when the time comes to consider the outcome of chemotherapy. He is discerning and says he will only operate if the tumour shrinks because it has wrapped itself around my celiac plexus like a pole dancer. It would be a ten-hour procedure involving a pancreatectomy and repair of the arteries. There is one major caveat. Once the tumour has metastasised, an operation of that severity is out of the question.

It buoys me thinking that my chances of reaching an operable state have increased. His interest in my case is proven by the fact that he promises he will take it to a multidisciplinary meeting at his hospital and examine the scans. A telehealth appointment is booked for a couple of days later.

Michelle and I sit at our usual spot at the kitchen table for Zoom calls, squeezed tightly together to fit our bodies in the frame. The surgeon begins by repeating the basic thrust of his approach. It is all a prelude to giving us unexpected news. One of the specialists at the multidisciplinary meeting, a radiologist, has noticed a dark spot on my liver that wasn't detected in earlier scans. The surgeon even puts up images of the scans to show us its appearance. What he is telling us is that this one minuscule spot is a sign of at least a single metastatic lesion. The message is clear. He can't say for certain that it's malignant, but he believes it to be so. He recommends an MRI, which proves his suspicions.

There is no way of spinning it. The rules of the battlefield have changed. The liver spot can now be seen by my oncologist retrospectively on scans. She says that it might have dated back to my initial diagnosis, though she can't be certain about this. The bad news is worse and, worse than worse, the spot has slowly been growing. I am put on a different chemotherapy regime. The cancer is in my bloodstream, so an operation is out of the question. I am now fighting two opponents. How long before they multiply and strike another organ? It is a knockout blow to my brain that I most fear.

The scales of life and death have dramatically tilted against my favour. I wonder if the physician who had earlier dismissed my complaints would finally be compelled to admit that he had found rat's balls on my scans.

In the Bible it says no man knows the time of his death. That's true, but there is an unbridgeable chasm between one who has a clear vision of the horizon of death to which they are fast approaching and those who know it as an abstract truism that we are all going to die one day. For me, the world has already divided into two. When I manage a ten-minute walk up the street, I feel a glass wall drop in front of me. I see that wall in the bustling streets on the regular drives to hospital like a child being driven by Mummy and pressing my face against the window to play 'I Spy', or when I go for a walk with Michelle and Melila past a pumping restaurant full of people.

I can sit for hours on a rocking chair bought for feeding Melila that has been repurposed by moving it next to the windows at the front of our apartment. I watch the crowds of thousands queue up for a concert at the Palais and recall going there with Michelle, not that long ago, to see Angus and Julia Stone, Hannah Gadsby, the Shins, Fleet Foxes and a highlight, taking our nephew to see *Star Wars* accompanied by the Melbourne Symphony Orchestra.

Our focus has dramatically switched from creating a new life to illness and death, the metamorphosis tangible in so many ways. Every time we go for an oncology appointment, we pass through a corridor that is connected to the maternity ward—the same one we attended for scans prior to the birth of Melila. The rooms of life and death literally share walls. The first time Michelle tried to call our oncologist to report that I'd developed a fever she was confused why the number that appeared on her phone was her obstetrician's. It took a few blinks of astonishment to realise that both doctors used the same pager service, and that the last time she had called that number was a few months earlier to inquire about whether her waters were breaking.

It would have been impossible for us to predict Michelle drawing on her injecting skills, developed from years of injecting herself during each IVF cycle, to inject me with morphine; or, after packing away the yellow sharps bins we'd used for her twenty-two cycles, bringing them out again to discard all the needles I require for pain relief.

The more I yearn for the ordinary routines of life, the greater I feel its impending loss. There is no way to escape awareness of my tumours. It pursues me relentlessly, filling every cell of my brain and body, day and night. As the physical pain lessens when the new chemotherapy regime starts to work, and the companion analgesics are gradually reduced, a different kind of pain sharpens. It operates on the principle of inverse proportion: the less the physical pain, the deeper the existential one.

As my physical condition improves, I try to shift my focus to a new paradigm.

I am living with cancer.

Melila, now almost ten months old, has moved quickly from commando crawling to sliding about the house and standing upright. My Melila loves her teddy bears, who sleep in her cot with her. She calls each of the treasured toys by names that Michelle and I chose for them, or rather for her. There is RBG (Ruth Bader Ginsburg), after the famous feminist jurist, who is a pair with Aharon Barak, the most distinguished judge in Israel's Supreme Court. Melila's mother blushes when I tell Melila how her mother clerked for Barak on the landmark targeted killing case. There's also Hannah Arendt so that my daughter will one day in the future be inspired to read her essays on statelessness, the banality of evil and radical responsibility; and JPS the frog, otherwise known as Jean-Paul Sartre, who teaches her a dose of existentialist philosophy. And she's learned to pronounce the name of her bunny, Yeshayahu Leibowitz, to remind her of the Jewish philosopher who never shied from calling out the crimes of occupation while sticking fast to his religious commitments. He understood that because of the imperative of a homeland for Jews, we have to be vigilant against turning the state, the nation, into an object of idolatry. Their worldviews, we hope, will seep into part of the value system we will try and instil in her and the next generation of my family clan.

She is an early speaker; she can name every member of her expansive family. She named herself Mimi and often refers to herself by her full name, Mimi Joni Baker. Michelle keeps a list of the words that are added daily to her vocabulary. Flower is one of her favourite words because, well, she loves picking flowers on our walks. Walk, initially pronounced 'worp', is another favourite word. Some things are named for the sensation it gives her. She calls a swing a wee-wee because it's the sound she makes as we push her, Michelle from the back, me from the front so I can steal the benefit of watching her smile.

Her mouth fills with teeth and she learns to count, at first the even numbers, leaving us to prompt her with the odd numbers. Soon she adds the words 'tablets' and 'hospital' to her vocabulary. She explores every corner of the house. While she loves her toys she prefers 'real' things, like picking items from the rubbish bins, or swiping the screens on our phones, sometimes calling random people or locking us out of our phones for a period of time. One of her favourite activities is twisting the lids on any kind of bottle or jar, which means we need to be extra careful with the countless medications spread across our house. 'Why won't she just play with puzzles?' we wonder as she explores an electricity outlet.

I am living with Melila, but I am always drawn back to the past by the laws that govern my life: the deeper the joy, the greater the pain.

I am living with cancer.

My eyes gravitate to the iconic Luna Park clown face and the lights that flicker over its giant smile. I am transported to a photograph taken inside the entrance behind the bared teeth of this gargantuan clown-king. My father is sitting on the moon against a blue starry night. Johnny is next to him, and I'm snuggled on my father's knee, about eight years old. Against the background screams of brave people propelled down the rattling wooden tracks of the Scenic Railway, I feel as if I'm sitting back on the moon beam with my father, Johnny, and squashed between us, Kerryn. Sometimes when I move my hands, I feel they are Johnny's hands, that I've embodied him like a puppet—twin souls, battling cancer.

And then the lights switch on and I see Michelle in the kitchen, singing and dancing with Melila, the only two people who can smash through that damn glass and touch me.

I buy Melila a present for her first birthday but I order it a month earlier because I'm fearful that any day my illness will take a sudden turn for the worse.

A baby grand piano.

When it is delivered, I place her on my knee and we hammer on the keys.

I allow myself to imagine my daughter as a concert pianist. I know they are fantasies. The plaque on the piano is deliberately ambiguous. It doesn't guilt her into moving beyond cacophonous banging. I don't allow myself to turn her into an abstraction. I call her my zisseh, Yiddish for sweetness, and use the name she has learned to associate with me for now, Dadda. That is all I can know—the present moment. The rest is imaginary, like writing fiction.

For my zisseh, Melila
May the music of life always flow through you
Love from your Dadda, forever.

I add the date of her first birthday on the plaque but then realise that we are already booked in for chemotherapy on that day.

Fortune smiles down on me. When I arrive at the hospital, the oncologist tells me my platelets are too low to withstand treatment. I'm free to leave.

We go to a children's farm together with Aunty Melila's twin nephews, Alva and Miro, and her sister Sarah, and pat the muddy sheep and goats. I revel in celebrating the present.

Sheep. Goats. And a dog.

'Woof,' Melila says.

I can tell already she's going to be a genius. A farmer and pianist, I laugh to myself.

My zisseleh. How my heart breaks and melts each day when I look at you. My love hurts so much I want to switch it off and turn away. But then I embrace you with wet eyes.

We are living with cancer.

Amid the grief comes good news. Rachel and her boyfriend, Joshua, drop by for a surprise announcement that they have decided to marry.

'We'd like you to officiate,' they say, knowing that I've conducted Jewish marriages.

Nothing could make me happier but I'm aware that the timing has been triggered by my illness. That isn't to say they are getting married for my sake. They have been a couple for seven years. The actual chuppah is held a month later in our home, designed to protect their immune-compromised father.

The shawl that covers the canopy was made by the groom's great-aunt and has witnessed numerous family weddings. Rachel asks if she can wear Kerryn's veil. I give her the ring Kerryn wore at our wedding. Gifted musicians from the Bashevis Singers agree to play for Rachel and Josh, the same sibling duo who played for Michelle and me on our wedding day. When they say it's a privilege, what they mean—once again—is that it's an honour to perform in light of the circumstances. Death is present even in my most joyous moments.

I lead Rachel down the aisle on my own, joined under the canopy by Michelle and Melila. The loudspeakers blare Kerryn's favourite song, audibly louder than the previous music—Carole King's 'Where You Lead'. It's as though Rachel believes that the volume will somehow bring her mother closer.

By the end of the ceremony, I am exhausted; I need to lie down in the break before dinner.

My mother's condition is worse. She can't stop shivering and a bed is made up for her. She doesn't emerge from the spare room, the grief overwhelming the joy at the marriage of the granddaughter she has always called her chandelier—her fire. She can no longer be fooled by my condition. She has seen the act twice before. And in the corner of our room is the gift that I have bought Melila with a plaque.

'Why is Marky buying such a big piano for Melila?' my mother asks Michelle.

Michelle doesn't answer.

My mother fills in the gaps. 'He must be preparing.'

She drags the bed cover over her head at her granddaughter's wedding and cries for the rest of the night.

22

—

THE PROSPECT of my death is pursued by the fear of another one.

'We can't risk leaving Melila an orphan,' I say to Michelle.

'I can't do the operation now,' she answers. 'I won't be able to lift Melila for weeks. Nor could I look after you.'

But we both know there is no choice, confirmed by our doctors, who urge us that now is the time for Michelle to remove her ovaries to protect her from developing a cancer as deadly as mine.

We call her doctor on a Friday and he fits her into his next operating list on Monday. After a panicked weekend of preparation and buying a spare foldout bed so that Yael can move into our home and help look after Melila, Michelle is admitted to hospital. We have decided to delay a full hysterectomy and limit the surgery to a bilateral salpingo-oophorectomy, an unfamiliar and strange-sounding procedure. It means that her fallopian tubes and ovaries will be removed, but her uterus kept and dealt with later.

Later. We use words casually, while harbouring the unspoken meaning of how they relate to my cancer.

By retaining her uterus, we also bypass the final and irreversible possibility of Michelle carrying a baby again. We decide that a decision about this now is too much to bear emotionally.

Less than six months after the operation, we make plans to implant the remaining embryos with my sperm and Michelle's eggs. We want Melila to know that we did everything to try to give her a sibling her age. We want to do this while my condition seems relatively stable, knowing of course that it can change at any moment. Dare we try for another miracle?

Our appointment with Kate happens to fall on our double anniversary—our wedding anniversary and Melila's implantation anniversary. We bring Melila to the appointment. She's fifteen months old and walks confidently into the doctor's rooms while the staff all coo over her.

We are realistic about our low chances of success and the added pressure on our lives in its current incarnation. If Michelle does become pregnant, I'm fully aware that it's unlikely I will be alive to witness the birth of a new child. Michelle asks how I feel about that possibility.

'Happy, even so,' I answer.

'For you or me?'

'Both of us,' I say, aware that there is neither happiness nor sadness in a grave.

During the first round Melila contracts hand, foot and mouth disease. It's a rite of passage for most toddlers and their parents, but for us it poses a number of risks. I am whisked away to spend a few nights at my mother's house for fear that I will catch it, which would delay chemo. As it happens, I end up in the ED anyhow, and then have a stint in hospital for a recurring chest infection that flares up and constantly interferes with my chemo schedule. Our other fear is that Michelle probably has it too. What risk will that be to the child we hope to conceive?

We consult Kate, who sets out clearly the pros and cons, leaving us to decide whether to delay the implantation until the following month.

'We can't delay,' I insist, knowing how quickly things might turn for me.

Michelle seems at first more unsure, but agrees without hesitation when I express my instinct firmly. Michelle has the embryo transfer while I am in hospital, and Melila is at home sick. For better or for worse, in our world of terminal cancer, the ten-day wait for the phone call informing us of the results isn't the focus of all our attention as it otherwise would have been. At first the levels of hCG are elevated, but they plummet after the next blood test. Another loss.

The following month we try again. Our last embryo. Michelle is prepped again with the hormones. On the day of the transfer, I walk to our local bookstore to buy Kate a couple of books I've managed to read recently. We enjoy talking books. But the books remain wrapped in the cupboard. We never go to the appointment. Kate calls Michelle, her voice low by contrast with its typical upbeat tone. There is no embryo to implant. She tells Michelle that it had started to disintegrate in the test tube when the scientist tried to thaw it.

Michelle is devastated. She can no longer avoid the fact that she will not have more children. She has largely repressed the grief over the removal of her ovaries because she had hoped that with her uterus intact, she could become pregnant again. The intensity of her anguish is compounded by the oestrogen and progesterone she is taking to keep her bones and general health intact after her ovaries were removed, the IVF medication and, of course, the increasingly clear signs that my condition is deteriorating. For me, the embryo transfers are a reminder of my limbo status between life and death. Half here, half not. And a reminder of the perverse world we inhabit, where my baby may be created, but I won't be around to see it or raise it. In contrast to the previous four years of our IVF journey, these embryo transfers take a remarkably secondary yet nonetheless extremely significant role because of the assault my body is under from the cancer and the chemo.

These thoughts trigger another conversation about the future, about later.

'I don't want you to be a widow for the rest of your life,' I finally say. 'You have more than forty years ahead of you. I want you to remember me after the grief eases, but I also want you to be free of me.'

'I don't want to ever be free of you.'

'The grief will ease, I promise you. I've been there before.'

'We're different,' she says. 'And anyway, you've never stopped grieving. You've suppressed it. And I'll have a child to bring up who will always be searching for her father.'

I think of the way Melila bangs on the bedroom door when Michelle takes her out in the morning and lets me sleep in.

'Dadda, Dadda,' she cries, and bursts into the room. Is that how she'll be for the rest of her life, not only as a baby but also a teenager and adult?

Michelle believes Melila will always want to know more about me. She uses my own adult kids as examples: they never stop asking questions about how Kerryn would have acted in a particular situation, how she would have guided them.

Michelle suggests I write notes for Melila that she can pass on to her at different stages of her life. One for each birthday. For her wedding. How else will she know her father?

I answer that I don't want to write to an abstraction. I can only give her Dadda, as I am now.

Michelle organises for us to do a tour of schools so that I can be part of the decision-making. For later.

We decide on a creche that we will send her to, the one her elder siblings attended. My kids break out into a repertoire of songs they remember from those early days. I want Melila to sing the same songs with them.

In my own way, I am hard at work shaping Melila's future. I talk to her about the books that influenced me. I don't consider Enid Blyton anachronistic or that the music I played on my record-player belongs to another era.

For now, I want Melila to encounter the same characters I remember from my youth. Moon-Face and the children who climbed the Faraway Tree and the fantastical sleuths in gangs of five and seven. I remember how I used to dress up as a detective and imagine with my cousin that there was a murder mystery we had to solve in our garden. I find a copy of *And Then There Were None*, which is also a description of my complete collection of Agatha Christie books that my mother threw away in one of her cleaning frenzies during my gap year, sparing only that single book.

I'm jolted back to reality. I am being nostalgic, projecting my own past onto her. How can I impose myself onto her future? Even my adult kids have carved out their own lives and values separate from my own.

How then can I mould Melila from the grave?

'We've got photographs,' I say to Michelle, who has been actively overusing her phone camera to capture my love for Melila, the way I read to her and whizz her in the air.

'The photos and videos aren't enough,' says Michelle. 'They'll stop one day,' she adds. She doesn't add the word 'soon', but we both know that I'll be lucky to survive to Melila's second birthday.

Two years. The formative years, according to most experts. I want to measure the dosage she will receive from me, like the label on one of my medications. Dadda: take twice daily or as prescribed by Mamma.

'It's you I want for Melila. Your voice. Your songs. Your passion for life.'

I make Spotify playlists for Melila. I agree to sing the religious tunes of festivals in my style and to record them. The elder kids have also asked me to do the same for them. I inscribe my favourite books from my shelves with memories of when I read them, as though I had authored them.

They all want to bottle me. To keep me forever.

That is precisely the deep pathos in what we are facing. I am going to die. And once I am gone, there is no way I can answer them from the grave. We are aware of the incoherent desire that is impossible to fulfil. My mind gropes for a German word that is used to describe how the generation born after the war had to do the 'memory work' of uncovering the past. *Vergangenheitsbewältigung.*

That's what Melila will be. An archaeologist, forever digging deeper and deeper into the hole inside her in the hope of finding what lies at the bottom of it. Or will her mother and siblings and my grandchildren be able to uncover forgotten memories? I imagine them sitting around a table or on a holiday, laughing about a story that concerns me. They take it in turns filling in the gaps.

It reminds me of one of my favourite lines from the Passover Seder. In retelling the story of the exodus from Egypt, our sages tell us that 'whoever expands on the story is to be praised'. Rather than offering a static version of myself in what I have self-consciously and selectively been leaving behind, I'd prefer them to feel free to reclaim their memories. To construct me as it seems truthful to them at their stages in life. To use their imagination and breathe me into the lives they build.

I can see them all bursting through my bedroom door calling out my name. 'Marky, Marky,' they all chant.

I don't answer but they can hear me, inside them, creating their response, expanding on the story, adding new pages and chapters.

For now, it's impossible to read past the present page. The words are smudged by Michelle's tears streaming down her face, as they do every night.

Michelle senses that my spirits are flagging. I'm lying in bed beyond my snoozes, or shloofs as I call them in Yiddish, and my mood is fluctuating. I barely see anyone outside the family, not even my closest friends. She encourages me to go out and meet up with friends and family eager to see me, or to go on a short daily walk to the new jetty at the beach. I had followed closely and with considerable excitement the protests when it was partially dismantled, and then its rebuilding. I joked that one day I'd run for mayor.

Or less ambitiously, she suggests, I could sit in my reading chair while Melila plays beside me with her toys. In different ways, but always gently, Michelle is pleading with me not to turn my back on the world.

Cautious optimism comes from a conversation that Michelle has with Cherie Dear, the wife of the famous footballer, Paul Dear, who had pancreatic cancer. She believes in the benefits of alternative medicine and claims that it has extended his life beyond all medical prognostications. I seek and receive from my oncologist permission to try some of these alternative practices.

First in line is a consultation with their naturopath. She specialises in integrative oncology and nutrition. As a result, my tablet bowl that Michelle fills from a Webster-pak triples in quantity. I am tempted to throw the new pills into the bin, especially the ones that don't come in capsule size and stick in my throat. But I'm impressed by the naturopath, who claims to prescribe medication to make my chemotherapy more effective. I consent to the enlarged dessert menu.

Next on the list is an acupuncturist—to boot, the same acupuncturist used by Paul Dear, whose boots won him a prestigious football medal. Again, I adopt the view that there's no harm in trying, not that I expect the needles to alter the outcome of my tumour. The acupuncturist I go to was trained in his birthplace of China and dresses in a thick traditional jacket with large laces that loop around the buttons. At first I wince as he places needles in the most unlikely of places, including my ears. For the next half-hour, cocooned in a blanket, I am instructed to close my eyes and sleep. I can't say I sleep or that I feel different when the needles are removed from my skin. But something about the words of the acupuncturist breaks through to me, and entices me to return of my own volition week after week. Speaking in a Chinese accent, his words sound banal, but in the context of my cancer they impact me profoundly.

'Your baby daughter is your heart. Your angel. She will heal you. The subconscious is very important. You must smile and believe.'

I carry his voice in my head, like Mr Miyagi in *The Karate Kid*.

'Remember. You can live with cancer. You are not a statistic. A tree can live with illness but we kill it when we try to cut out the disease with an axe. You are an ancient tree. You must stop thinking you are dying.'

My embrace of his words might be an act of desperation. I know the statistics but at the same time no person is a statistic. Most importantly, the acupuncturist treats me as a person, an individual with cancer. He takes the time to learn about the people in my family circle who love me. All this contrasts with most of the oncologists and doctors, who barely know my name without looking at my latest tumour markers on the computer screen. They treat me like someone who makes it onto the rollcall: Name. Date of birth. Address.

To them, I am a patient who falls within a mean distribution of possible outcomes. I have never expected miraculous promises but I yearn for dignity. The bureaucratic administration of doctors who take on too many patients channels a familiar source of anger, an appendix to the months when I was misdiagnosed. I won't be silent this time. I want my team of doctors to fight for the one per cent chance that I can be an outlier.

The result of my CT scan, four months after my diagnosis, brings encouraging news. I am responding well to the chemotherapy, or rather the tumours on my pancreas and liver are responsive.

Michelle urges me to be positive. 'Every week counts. Look at how much Melila changes every day.'

I know she is right but I can't accept the celebratory mood. I want thirty years. All my positive vibes and people's prayers can't change the inevitability that the chemo will one day stop working its magic, and abracadabra, the tumours will zip through my body. I turn to my doctors and beg them to find me a trial—here or overseas in the United States.

The response: 'It's unlikely you'll be eligible for a trial and, in any case, phase one or two trials will unlikely impact your condition.'

'I don't care,' I answer. 'It's my only hope.'

Chemotherapy is a dead end for me, literally. Even the radiation oncologist I initially consult tells me that he will only intervene when I am in pain again—that is, for palliative treatment.

All I have are the words of the acupuncturist. 'Your baby daughter is your healer. You can live with cancer.' And our weekly motto, as he sticks a needle into my ear.

'Thirty years,' he repeats like a mantra. 'There are angels in your family who love you.'

'Thirty years,' I answer, surrendering reason for a deep yearning to believe my tumour understands the meaning of my love story with Michelle.

The following week when I go to acupuncture, I ask him if he's heard the news.

After an awkward silence, he nods forlornly, almost apologetically.

'But he lived for twenty-two months. More time than the doctors gave him.'

We don't mention Paul Dear's name as he sticks needles in my ears.

Soon after, I move to a different oncologist, who begins each consultation by setting aside the scans and blood results and asking how I, Mark Baker, feel that day. I sense he can see me and will fight for every extra day. At last, a presiding doctor I can surrender to, who puts me on high-dose targeted radiotherapy alongside my chemotherapy in the hope that my longevity can be improved.

Longevity. When I hear the word, I think of the biblical character Methuselah, who lived 969 years. For me, the story of his lifespan is fanciful, a reminder that all my treatment is palliative rather than curative.

Still, I keep taking the vitamins and going to weekly acupuncture sessions. I want to believe in the angels who love me.

I imagine that love will be enough to face my end.

Ten months.

That's the figure that sticks in my head. It's how long Kerryn lived. It's how long Johnny lived. I am stuck on their karma wheel.

Do I count from December when I first had my CT or from my date of diagnosis? CT or MRI, that is the question.

The date haunts me. I pass my use-by date based on the first scan. And then I reach summer. Eight months.

My single liver metastasis has started growing by several millimetres at each scan. If it doesn't stop, soon I'll be chopped liver. During this period, I try to squeeze in good times, to follow the orders to change my outlook and live with my cancer. I gather the tribe—my adult kids, their partners and my grandchildren, and Michelle and Melila. And me.

A friend has generously offered us their holiday house in Daylesford, the same place I'd gone to when The Pain began, the same area I'd contemplated buying a holiday house. It's only two hours from my hospital in Melbourne.

But I'm not the same traveller. We're blessed with a few warm days at the end of winter, but the chemotherapy has chilled my bones. I huddle next to heaters, wrap myself in jackets and blankets and watch from a distance as the family cooks barbecues outdoors, and plays board games. Dadda/Zaida—Zaidad—lies on a built-in trampoline surrounded by bush, and I flex my body to let the bubs around me experience the sensation of bouncing. After three days, I tell Michelle I need to go home. The following day the skies open and release a biblical deluge around the holiday house we had fled.

The next holiday is more successful. The same configuration, plus my mother, head off on a plane to the hot summer climate of Byron Bay in northern New South Wales. We stay in a rainforest, each with our own rooms. I spend roughly half my time in the bathroom, the other half enjoying family time: walks to the adjacent beach where the dogs outnumber their owners, and which provides plentiful opportunities for Melila to woof back at them. We picnic on the grass, go for dinners and I swim laps of the pool, kicking my neuropathic feet which feel like they have weights attached to them. I emerge from the pool proud of myself, but self-conscious of the robotic look of the port protruding from my chest, reminiscent of *Milton the Monster*, a TV series I watched as a kid.

All the while, I have a stomachache, one that resembles the band of tightness and bloating I experienced when my pancreas began to manifest itself. I've been told by the doctors that it's malabsorption and been given a range of recipes to make up for the lack of enzymes that give purpose to the evolutionary life of our pancreas. It's impossible to find the right balance of medications but it doesn't matter, I'm surrounded by love and playfulness and on the way to beating the race past the ten-month post. If I make it, I let myself think, I can live forever.

While no number of deaths could make me indifferent to what awaits me, watching a sequence of deaths in the family has made me more prepared. I feel as though I have been trained or mentored in the art of dying. My fear is less the prospect of my ultimate demise than the pain I will endure reaching the end.

What haunts me most about dying is the deep knowledge I've gained about the suffering of those who will 'survive' me. Most of all Michelle, whose protestations of strength are uttered for my sake only. She tries to hide the cracks in her demeanour. They can't be hidden. They are clearly visible to her dentist, who asks if she has been experiencing stress these past few months. Michelle is puzzled by the question, which seems more appropriate for a psychologist to ask. He shows her an X-ray from before my diagnosis and compares it to the present. The dentist is shocked by how her teeth have cracked from clenching in such a short period. And her first pair of reading glasses, acquired after I became ill, needed to be rectified by several stops only two months later.

'How can that happen so quickly?' Michelle asks the optometrist and dentist.

The same answer: stress and fatigue.

Who would have thought that a set of well-preserved teeth and spectacles could be a synecdoche for the radical turnaround in the roots of Michelle's life?

My mother wails through the phone how much she loves me, Michelle and Melila. I tell her that we love her too. She wants to care for me as though I have never ceased to be her Markinu, to cut my nails as she used to and, perhaps, to sprinkle eau de cologne on my sick bed.

When Melila was born my mother would say that she is a gift from God. Now she has started saying, 'Melila is a gift from you.'

My terminal illness has paradoxically given me omnipotent powers. But the subtext is clear: what my mother means is that Melila is my parting gift to buoy those who survive me, particularly herself and Michelle.

I recall vividly how courageous my mother was when she visited the hospice where Kerryn died, and wouldn't let go of her hand. My father could only peek through the door at the daughter-in-law he loved, blinking away his tears. It was time for them to leave the hospice but my mother refused, and glued herself onto a couch in front of a gas fire until it was dark; exactly as it would be, twenty months later, when she was forced to unwrench herself from Johnny.

My mother had chosen Johnny's name from a 1950s song, 'Johnny Is the One for Me'. He had put on a brave face for our parents as the cancer burrowed deep into his bones. He procrastinated telling them he was dying, and pretended that he was on the road to healing. My father dissembled along with him, always the one to avoid confrontation and to appease others. My mother knew, and in private cried to anyone who would listen. But nothing could prepare us for that moment when she approached his hospital bed that had been installed among his library of books and CDs, and she stroked his piano fingers, caressing them and heaving as though she was going to collapse and die in his place. Expressing the wish to die in his place. That's what she yowled at Kerryn's and Johnny's funerals, doctors on standby in case she collapsed. We had witnessed the unthinkable image of my father digging into muddy sand, tossing it into his son's grave, like the little boy in the slave labour camps.

My mother never adjusted after Yossl died. They'd been married for sixty-seven years. She had been totally dependent on him, and of all the deaths, it was his that affected her life the most. Since his death, she sits for hours in her garden patch with its water fountain, chain-smoking cigarettes and talking to her dead husband. When we returned to Surfers to pack up the apartment we sold after thirty years of holiday leisure, she banged on the front door, screaming out his name, as if she might find him lying on his recliner chair, his blue dressing gown unstrapped, his undies exposed.

Three graves in five years.

One more is added ten months later: my mother's sister, Sylvia, twelve years her junior, with whom I joked that we're competing in a race to the finishing line.

I watched her die, her hospital bed lowered to the floor as though she was mourning herself in the traditional Jewish posture meant for family survivors. My mother stroked her arm, soothing her with memories of their childhood in Berlin, the death of their mother at the end of the war and how my mother had tried her best to fill the gap by acting as a substitute mother. Could my Aunty Sylvia hear her sister's consolations, or was she already unconscious, in a place beyond words?

What will be the last word that I will hear?

MammaDadda.

There is a time for everything. A time for life and nurturing. Ours has been a season of death punctuated by glimpses of profound fecundity. A family whose head and soul has been lacerated. The Bekiermaszyn and Krochmal clan from Poland and Ukraine.

If I could film the last seven years of my life, I would call it *Four Funerals and a Wedding*. My marriage to Michelle has transcended all of these deaths, stood outside of them, but was also framed by them through an act of pure love. Love of Michelle and of the baby we created, a love which will soon be snatched from us by a fifth funeral.

Who will narrate this new script after I am gone? I wonder how long before Melila will realise Dadda isn't in the bedroom and call out for Mamma only, and experiment with ways to tell the story of her missing father.

MammaDadda.
Dadda. Dadda.
Mamma.
Mamma.
Once upon a time …

23

WE ALL know in our heads that one day we will die. Naively, we believe that such knowledge somehow prepares us for the dreaded moment when we learn that the end is closer. Or at least I did. Rather foolishly, I fantasised that I would set up a tent in the Judean desert, go on a hunger strike and wait until a final peace accord was signed between Israelis and Palestinians. I knew it was a piece of shticky melodrama, but some part of me wished to believe that my one last vainglorious tilt at living would be an act of megaphone martyrdom.

Was it the circumstances in which I imagined facing my own death—witnessing the deaths of Kerryn and Johnny—that explains my lack of insight? In awe of their dignity, did I somehow believe that it would be my political convictions that would define me as inspiring to the end?

Naively (again) I did not imagine I would get to test myself so soon. I quickly learned that what is important to me narrowed into a series of concentric circles at whose core lies my family, followed by close friends. Almost all my thoughts and actions are for Michelle, my children, my mother and my grandchildren, and the pain of witnessing their grief and carrying mine.

Even fantasies of grand political acts and small ones now exist outside my orbit. It's difficult to explain what it's like to believe that it's unlikely that one has a future. In my new inner world of chemotherapy, radiotherapy, nurses and oncologists, I have become unresponsive to almost everything I once cared about passionately—the political state of the world, ideological debates, the doomsday news cycle fed to me by the second on social media. The only news that preoccupies me is my tumour markers. My world has shrunk and pushed the things that mattered most to me out of my mental frame. I've lost interest in seeing friends, my photography, the legacy of Trump's reign of terror.

History is too abstract for me when my breath is short, and time is short. It's not that the issues aren't important to me or that I minimise my past obsessions with them. I still consider the occupation regime in Israel–Palestine to be deeply unjust, and that as a Jew, and an identifying Zionist, I am implicated in the tragedy of the settlement enterprise and the oppression of Palestinians. I will go to my grave with those beliefs, and sadness that in my life I never got to see Israel transformed into a state built on its foundational principles of justice.

But the passion and even the hope has gone. As I stare into the wilderness of knowing and not knowing my future in the home that Michelle has made for me and Melila, my focus is on injecting as much of 'me' as I can into the people I love. All that matters is staring into the sum-total of my life and reconciling myself to its blessings and flaws. Now is not the time to belatedly try to fit in all the things I always wanted to do, as if in the eleventh hour you can define who you are and the life you have lived.

My struggle now is to get out of bed and to play with Melila, or to see my grandchildren and walk down the street with them. I barely recognise my disfigured body. I have shaved my hair, lost my muscle weight, lightened my olive skin.

Who am I?

It leaves me wondering about the question posed by Reb Zusia. Have I been Mark Baker? Truthfully, authentically myself? True to myself?

I don't even know how to construct a narrative of my life outside of the bits and pieces of my years.

My friends have noticed the way my interests and projects have shifted each decade of my life. Drained of the daily toil and deliberations that made their realisation possible, they now feel like a bronze statue marking my legacy. My academic career. The books I have written. The Jewish journal I edited. The organisation for global social justice I founded. The synagogue I established and led. My role as director of Jewish studies.

If there is one action that expresses what I hope is an essential aspect of my true self, it is my response to the cynical claim that refugees from Afghanistan stranded at sea en route to Australia were throwing children overboard. How is it possible, I asked myself, that while these lies about desperate people were being spread, the leaders of my Jewish community were organising a gala event to honour the man who aggressively promoted those dehumanising policies, Prime Minister John Howard?

On a whim, I bought a sheet of cardboard and texta and in large letters wrote 'ST LOUIS 1939', referring to the shipload of Jewish refugees who were turned back from Havana to Europe, where they were consumed by the Holocaust. Beneath it I wrote 'EXODUS 1947', referring to the ship of postwar refugees immortalised by the Leon Uris novel I read as a teenager, and the film starring Paul Newman. And in bold letters I added the name of the ship, 'TAMPA 2001', that was being denied entry to Australia.

I held up my placard, alone in a sea of Jewish communal leaders, who laughed at me as though I was a clown in a Fellini movie.

'I'll cut your balls off,' one mogul said. I then stared into the bevy of press cameras following the Prime Minister into the hall and left with my placard when the doors of the hall were closed to me. I saw myself as honouring the memory of many brave people who protested against world indifference to the fate of Jews during the Holocaust.

Which am I?

A self-made hero or a circus clown, pitiful, scorned, rendered (suitably) invisible in the following days by the felling of the twin towers in Manhattan, that multiplied the scorn for my narcissistic antics?

But one weekend, twelve months into my illness, between a doctor's appointment and a shloof, I answered the question: shaken out of apathy, out of my weariness of spirit, by my love for Melila, I dragged myself to my local protest against the judicial coup in Israel with her and Michelle. We armed Melila with the teddies we had named in honour of judicial integrity—RBG and Aharon Barak. Michelle took a photo. I hope that when I am gone, she will show it to my baby daughter and tell her what was important to us, and what it means to be a citizen of the world who can stand up for what they believe in, even when their spirits are low and they're left only with their will to take them where principle says they must go.

My bookshelves are filled with subjects that tell a meta-story about my shifting interests over the decades: Polish Jewish studies, history of terrorism, social anthropology, postcolonial theory, Haskalah literature, Yiddish castaways. They are overshadowed by the fiction section that allures me; the books unread, and the books read in my youth. I find myself drawn to those novels and authors from my final years at school, perhaps in a futile attempt to relive and return to those years where the future lay ahead of me. Graham Greene's *The Power and the Glory* and *The Heart of the Matter*, which reflect on faith and sin, and also death. Rather than the frustrating chase to keep up with contemporary books, I want time to reread *Sons and Lovers*, *The Go-Between* and Margaret Drabble's *The Millstone*. And then there are the Russian novels I studied in their original black-spined Penguin editions at university. Do I have time for *Anna Karenina*, *War and Peace*, the books by Turgenev and stories by Chekhov? Does anyone have time? And what of Virginia Woolf, Steinbeck and all of Philip Roth and Bernard Malamud, as though I've never met their characters, or alter egos in Roth's case? Henry Roth's *Call It Sleep* is in my top ten books of six decades' worth of reading. And *To Kill a Mockingbird*. So too is Wallace Stegner's *Crossing to Safety*, which I've already read three times. Still, I long to read it again, with new eyes, and with the weight of a deviant pancreas. And what of the classics unread on my shelf: Michelle's copy of *Middlemarch* and *Remembrance of Things Past*? Do I have time to read all these books in my lifetime? Would I ever have read them if I'd lived till old age?

My musical taste has shifted to mirror my literary preferences. I've returned to classical music, though I still love the folk singers of the politically conscious decades: Bob Dylan, Joni Mitchell, Carole King, James Taylor. In my bedroom during my university days I hung a large poster of Bach above my record-player. I now lie in bed at night wearing AirPods and listen to everything Bach, especially his *Cello Suites*; Mozart's *Requiem*; Strauss' *Metamorphosen* and Mahler's Adagietto from *Symphony No. 5*, used to great effect in the movie rendition of Thomas Mann's *Death in Venice*. Perhaps it's the theme of plague, and the final scene where

Dirk Bogarde falls into the Great Sleep reclining on a deckchair on a Venetian beach. I have mostly stopped listening to other music, except for the Wiggles, who endlessly entertain Melila, and 'The Happy Song'. She also listens to Vivaldi's *Four Seasons* and waves her fingers like a conductor. I imagine her playing the baby grand piano I bought for her on her first birthday that carries a plaque from her Dadda.

I know I must dig deeper to answer the question posed by Reb Zusia. Perhaps there is a buried psychic drama that can peel off the layers of who I am, one that links my cancer to my mother's trauma. The hole in which she was buried. Her claim that her depression began when I almost died as a baby from croup. Pleading for my life, as she had once pleaded for hers when she was caught by a Nazi officer. Her overreaching ambition and the way she categorised my brother and me.

My brother was the strong one—defiant, brilliant and independent. It took another five years for her to gather the strength to bear another child. From the moment I was born, I was the weak one and when, after my illness, I survived, I became a mirror image of her. Weak, sickly, spoiled. I was in need of constant care by my father, by matron in school, by her when I was sent home and was tucked into her double bed to recover, again and again, from stomach pains.

The dynamic was established. As I grew, I looked up to my brother. He was my hero, my role model. When he dropped out of medicine to live in Israel, I became an only child for the remaining six years of my school years. After graduating, I wanted to follow in his footsteps. I spent my gap year in Israel in 1978, started in a Yeshiva but defected because the conditions were too spartan. I eventually found my way to the Hebrew University. I wanted to stay in Israel, and to be a soldier like my brother became when he enlisted in the 1982 Lebanon war. But my mother flew to Israel to wrench me away—not Johnny, who could defy her, but me, her alter ego, who belonged at home.

At home I plotted my rebellion. I joined a socialist youth movement, grew my hair long, dropped out of law school before the first year began, and pursued an arts degree. My plan was to return to Israel and become a teacher. Like my brother. But my trajectory took me further than my original intentions and carved a fork in the road. After completing my honours year in History I longed to become an academic. The next two years were spent in Oxford studying Jewish history, fuelled by fantasies drawn from *Brideshead Revisited* that were very different from my Israel dreams.

A small diversion: I went ahead of Kerryn for the first semester while she completed her medical degree. Orphaned after our marriage, she lived with my parents in Johnny's empty room. Where Johnny had always been the magnet that pulled me in his direction, she became the source of a new kind of ambition that pushed me towards career success. After two years living a life of Wensleydale cheese and port on a dreamy stage set of medieval spires, we moved to Israel. Johnny and Anita had returned to Australia and he entered my father's business, a form of work that he shunned and treated as a pastime while he channelled his frustrated ambitions into communal activism.

Kerryn and I moved into Johnny's Jerusalem home, slept in his bedroom, while I worked on my Oxford doctorate in his study. I walked the same route in his footsteps up the wadi adjoining his street to the Hebrew University, where I conducted my research in its library. Gabe was born and we returned to Australia after I was offered a position as the inaugural lecturer in Jewish history at the University of Melbourne. It was a case of sliding doors, or perhaps trading places. When I wrote *The Fiftieth Gate* about my parents' Holocaust experiences, it was as though I was claiming their story. In biblical terms, it was a Jacob and Esau saga, the younger son stealing the elder son's birthright.

None of this fit with my mother's narrative. She took pride in my academic triumphs, but in her mind Johnny was the clever one, the one who was meant to be a doctor. 'He could have been anything,' she always says and continues to say, 'a lawyer, a judge, a politician', perpetuating a rivalry between us even after his death.

I am a dreamer, a *luftmensch* with my head in the clouds, antagonising powerful people with my political antics. Johnny, by contrast, always knew how to win people over. Perhaps these parallel and divergent paths are the deeper structures that make up my story. In authorial terms, they take on an omniscient or third-person perspective, for my role has not been forged by my own wilful intentions. My mother is the main protagonist, pulling the strings that make up her sons' psychological attributes, drawing two brothers into close but duelling protagonists. 'The Fabulous Baker Boys', we were called in an article in the Jewish press. And for our last act, horrifically unpredictable but consistent with a prewritten script, our lives have merged: as in the beginning, I am following him to his grave. We both have been stricken by upper gastrointestinal cancers. We are dying at exactly the same age. When I hear myself laughing, I hear his voice. It is as though I have embodied his flesh. He has become my dybbuk, the spirit that lies inside me, speaking through me, determining the length of my prognosis, two sons merging into one, over which my mother can no longer imagine a life beyond. Indeed, when she threatens to kill herself, though she won't, it would be the fitting end to an operatic melodrama. Madame Butterfly comes to mind. Madame Bakermachine.

How can I determine the truth of my story? I am like a book by William S Burroughs. My life can be cut into pieces and assembled in different ways, or is like a pack of cards that I can see my father shuffling before randomly dealing them out. A full house looks different each time. There is no linear story, or discrete chapters. There is no Before or After. There is only the projection of what was and what might have been: memory—fickle, pliant, circular, fragmentary.

My beginning is my end. A child as an adult. An adult as a child. Riding the circle game until I am gone, leaving the detritus of my life to be picked up and told, and retold, by those who summon up my name. Dust to ashes. Ashes to dust.

That is why I have asked my family to etch a particular image onto my tombstone. It is the clock that sits on the belfry of the oldest synagogue in Prague, appropriately known as the AltNeu Shul—the Old–New Synagogue. The Hebrew letters from one to twelve mark out time. They have been inscribed backwards, so that one o'clock is eleven o'clock. Or perhaps, because Hebrew script is read from right to left, the hands of time tick anticlockwise. Even to one versed in the Hebrew alphabet, the Prague clock is disorientating, Kafkaesque, even though it was installed a thousand years before the birth of the modernist writer.

My children have told me they will also tattoo this image onto their bodies after I am gone. If my blood platelets weren't low, I would do the same now.

The clock is ticking, forwards and backwards. Soon, time will stop for me and the putrid water from which I was formed will merge with the worms and maggots in my grave. I will be the one person at my burial who doesn't hear the thud of earth landing on the coffin or note who was present (and absent) from the funeral of the late Mark Baker, to which he added the middle name Raphael, after his oldest ancestor and the angel of healing.

Who is Mark Raphael Baker?

I dream I arrive in an unknown place. A lorry with a taxi sign pulls up, with three unidentifiable drivers. I instruct them to take me home but we get lost on concrete highways. I try to guide them to familiar streets but we divert onto a long stretch of road with a dead end that is the ocean. The next thing I am transported to a village where all the shops are signposted Bakermachine, my father's family name from before the war in Poland, before he shortened it to Baker. I see my father dancing with a relative who has just declared they have COVID.

'You won't be able to see Melila,' I scold my father, and then I wake up, confused, like reading a book that I'll never finish.

I drag myself out of bed. Michelle helps me dress Melila. I want to stroll the same route I used to take before I was diagnosed. All we can hear is the warble of morning birds. I continue towards the beach and wait for the traffic lights to show the green walking person. I feel jealous of the early morning joggers. I used to run a five-kilometre stretch along the beach a couple of times a week. My dream from before Melila was born was to run with her in a sturdy jogger pram.

Shattered dreams, when you are facing death, become bucket lists, and this one edges high on the list. My kids buy me a second stroller for Melila, a three-wheeler designed for long-distance sprinting. But when I try it, I can barely accelerate for more than thirty seconds. My neuropathic feet and legs are too weak to carry me, and my breath is too short to speed up. I cross off the item on my bucket list. At least I tried. Give yourself a tick.

I take the route towards the ocean along a new viewing platform called the Circle of Reflection. When I look at the sea, something stirs in me. It is the sea inside me. When I was misdiagnosed with IBS, I had listened to hypnotherapy recordings in the bath. One of the visualisations was the ocean passing through my intestines, removing the stones that were causing me pain. There is no chance of the sea doing that but it awakens within me a deep longing for life.

I take Melila to the edge of the pontoon and point at the seagulls dipping into the bay. I point beyond, past the horizon, at the endless ocean. Somewhere on a distant island the water splashes along the edge of the earth. I imagine myself travelling there on a boat, through night and day to where the wild things are. On the other side I see a mirror image of myself standing on the edge of the railing with Melila.

I stare out at the ocean again and tears well in my eyes. I bend down and kiss Melila on the cheek.

'Dadda's okay,' she says to me.

She reaches out and wipes my tears. How does she know to comfort me? I am overwhelmed by how much I love this world. Perhaps because death has visited me so often these past years, I have skipped a stage of mourning. Denial. I have an exit strategy. The survivors are the ones who will suffer.

Looking at the sea, I don't want that exit strategy. I want to anticipate a future, an afterlife as in the poem by the Moroccan mystic of the sixteenth century, Avraham Azulai:

Just as in Genesis,
God breathed a soul
into a human body
to create the first human being,
So, at death,
the human soul
breathes itself
into God's body.

Have I let my zealous atheism tame my fears of the oblivion of death? Defeat me?

I have no illusions.

The high odds are that by the end of the year—earlier?—I will no longer be here. I don't know when that time will come. Right now, I feel a life force bleed in me, my soul breathes through me. My fatigue wants to fight it, but I say to myself, I can fight back. I don't have to live in the Kingdom of the Ill. I don't have to accept death. I can live with my tumour, the healing treatments of chemotherapy, the dice cast against me. I can also live with the irrational hope that drove Michelle to continue with IVF cycles until we created our miracle baby. I don't expect a miracle, but I can act as if it will come, just like love came crazily in my path and I picked myself up from the ground so that Michelle would stand by my side for the rest of my life, forever.

I make sure the brakes on Melila's three-wheel stroller are activated. I know I can do it. During my season of death, I went on a yoga retreat to the Greek islands and told the instructor I had one aim. There was no rational reason, but I wanted to stand on my head. Each time I stumbled until finally I learned to do a tripod head stand.

After I was diagnosed with cancer, Michelle organised a private yoga class at home on my birthday. I loved it so much that the teacher returned each week, then twice a week. It's the only thing that gets me out of my head and allows me to forget that I have cancer, this single hour on the mat. I tell the teacher that my aim is to once again stand on my head and see the world upright—my upside-down world.

I go down on all fours onto the hard floor of the pier. I know I should have a rubber mat but the risk of falling on wood spurs me on. I place my arms outwards and kick my feet up. They fall back on the ground. I try again. The same thing. On the third attempt, I feel my body rise, the tumour and liver spot stretching inside me, and for one millisecond I am suspended in the air. I wonder what Melila is thinking, watching her Dadda upside-down. And then I fall hard on the ground onto my back. The back that has been screaming for pain relief.

I lie there for a few seconds and look up at the vaulted sky.

Rain has begun to fall lightly.

I pull myself up and unlock the brakes on Melila's wheels. I sing her a Yiddish song that my father used to sing to me, and me to my children, and now my mother to Melila. I turn the masculine words into the feminine. I dare myself to dream about my baby's future.

Go to sleep my beautiful girl,
Close your little dark eyes
A little girl who already has all her teeth
Still needs her Dadda to sing her a lullaby.

The skies open and whip us with torrential rain. I push my daughter homeward and protect my sweet Melila, my zisseleh, by picking up speed.

Am I really running?

POSTSCRIPT

Michelle Lesh and Raimond Gaita

We, Mark's widow and his stepfather-in-law, prepared Mark's manuscript for publication during the twelve months that followed his death. The experience was sometimes surreal, sometimes cathartic, but always heart-wrenchingly painful.

Mark died on 4 May 2023, thirteen months after he was diagnosed with pancreatic cancer. During his first night in hospital, he wrote notes on his laptop, responding to the many echoes that the meaning of his illness had for him. He was in the same hospital in which his first wife, Kerryn, and his brother, Johnny, had been treated for cancer. Kerryn had died seven years before, and Johnny less than two years after her. His sensibility was deeply formed by scholarly and spiritual engagement with biblical texts. Ecclesiastes 3:1–8 came naturally to mind: 'To everything there is a season; a time to be born, and a time to die.' He came to think that the season of death he endured as a mourner would now extend until it encompassed his own. When he was discharged from hospital almost a month later, he resolved to write a memoir. For most of his adult life being a writer had been part of his conception of himself. Now the need to write was urgent—to record his thoughts and feelings and to understand them. Above all, he wanted to write for his daughter Melila, who was eight months old at the time.

Over the course of his illness Mark wrote almost every day, despite the ravages and the debilitating side effects of his treatments, which often left him weary in body and mind. Writing the memoir was an act of love that took possession of him. It gave him comfort and energy. He sacrificed sleep, physical and mental rest, and refrained from engaging with people and aspects of the world to which he had previously given so much of himself. This was his gift to Melila; through this book she could come to know him and learn of his love for her and the joy she gave him during the bleakest period of his life. It was also a gift for his family, most especially to his adult children, born to Kerryn. He hoped that hearing his voice in it, they would feel close to him and find comfort in that.

Michelle had read previous drafts many times. Ironically, though he was a historian, accuracy regarding dates and timeframes often eluded him. The three of us went over in close detail what transpired to be the penultimate draft. He produced another draft in response, which we expected to discuss with him, but his condition declined too rapidly.

We were left with a manuscript that was an astonishing moral and artistic achievement. It contained much fine, often haunting, writing; its closing lines searingly beautiful. In his portrait of his mother, Genia, Mark created a character who will live long in the memory of readers. She is like a modern-day biblical Naomi, who lost her husband and two sons, dubbing herself Mara (bitter) because her life was bitter through disappointment. Mark's depiction of her suffering will ache in the hearts of all his readers.

Mark entrusted us with completing the manuscript. The narrative ends where Mark wanted it to. No major sections were missing, but it required considerable work before it could be presented to a publisher. We finished sentences left hanging and clarified ones whose meaning was opaque. Occasionally we added entire paragraphs when it was evident that, either hurried or distracted, Mark felt the need to push the narrative along before the next chemotherapy session. Michelle trawled through his notes to her, and mini drafts, to help us in our efforts to ensure that as many of Mark's words as possible appeared in our additions. As all editors do, we cut and added, but unlike professional editors, we could not take what we had done to the author for discussion on those suggested changes. We had to trust that our intimate knowledge of Mark justified what we believed he intended to say when he did not say it. There were occasions when we could not be sure; sometimes it was problematic even to apply the concept of intention. We then relied on context and coherence to decipher what he meant; sometimes we left ambiguities unresolved, which is true to how life often is.

Some books, JM Coetzee wrote, 'read like [ones] that miraculously write themselves, that use their author simply as a medium to be born into the world'. Mark was a writer intuitively attuned to the resonances of literary and religious texts as he heard them emerge for him from deep in our cultural history. They were his Muse and he trusted their inspiration. We had, therefore, to be open to discovering aspects of him we did not know that had emerged in the process of writing *A Season of Death*, aspects that might have surprised even him.

The cuts we made were to prevent unwanted repetitions, to facilitate the flow of the narrative or because sentences or occasionally paragraphs were unclear, making us doubtful that we could reconstruct their meaning. Conscious that Mark hoped the book would be a work of literature, we never cut if doing so would undermine that hope. Nor did we ever cut to protect him from critical responses to his ethical opinions or his portrayal of people or events. Always, our overriding concern was to be faithful to the manuscript. We knew he expected this of us, without compromise. He had told Rai, 'You can't write a memoir looking over your shoulder.'

Ecclesiastes is the principal epigraph for *A Season of Death*. Its melancholy wisdom often suffuses its tone. Yet, this is a book written by a man whose spirit was lit by humour, who was urbanely attached to the world and who, above all, possessed a love of life that all who knew him prized. The appearance of paradox dissolves if one considers that love of life takes at least two forms. One is permeated through and through by knowledge of one's mortality. It is given, Mark says in his commentary on Reb Zusia, only to those who are facing death and whose understanding of themselves as essentially mortal creatures is not just in their heads, but lodged firmly in their hearts, with no possibility or even the desire to retreat from there. To do so, we think Mark believed, would be to forsake one's humanity. The other is a love of life in which such an understanding of mortality is at least faint when it is not absent.

Mark moved from one to the other. The second called to him from the 'land of the living' to cease mourning, to allow himself to fall in love with Michelle and to start a new family at the age of fifty-seven. One can hear it in the tone of his bewilderment, verging on incredulity, when he was told he had cancer, as though he had been hubristically confident that he would live a long time because it was owed to the Baker family, who had been acquainted with death too often. But when he knows his death is imminent and he says he must turn again to Reb Zusia to ask, 'Have I been Mark Baker?', his love of life was transformed into the first kind. Imbued with the integrity of his response to the wisdom of Reb Zusia, it required him to live his dying as the most authentic version of himself. That, rather than the conscious attempt to do so, enabled him to die with a calm grace and dignity.

ACKNOWLEDGEMENTS

It would have given Mark joy to know that Foong Ling Kong would edit *A Season of Death* and publish it. Years before she became publisher at MUP, she had championed his memoir, *Thirty Days*, and earned his unreserved trust in her editorial judgement and in her ear for his voice as they worked together on the manuscript. Her inwardness with his spirit and her enthusiasm for, as she put it, 'bringing Mark's last dance to fruition', eased our pain while we worked on the manuscript, hearing him anew each time we turned to it. By placing the production of the book into the wise and creatively assured hands of Catherine McInnis, Foong Ling guaranteed that Mark could not have found a better, more welcoming home for it.

Eugenie Baulch copyedited with sensitivity, precision and a fine ear for tone that inspired our admiration.

Anita Lester designed the wonderful cover art. Rich with symbolism and juxtapositions, it converted into art her understanding of the essential elements of the book's content and what was uniquely and characteristically Mark. It brought happiness to Mark in his final days.

Krystyna Duszniak encouraged him to continue writing the memoir. She was his reader, as she had been with his previous books. He trusted her sharp eye for detail and was grateful for her unwavering support.